SHALAMA
MY 96 SEASONS IN CHINA

JEAN HOFFMANN LEWANDA

Shalama: My 96 Seasons in China

By Jean Hoffmann Lewanda

ISBN-13: 978-988-8843-77-0

© 2024 Jean Hoffmann Lewanda

BIOGRAPHY & AUTOBIOGRAPHY

EB218

All rights reserved. No part of this book may be reproduced in material form, by any means, whether graphic, electronic, mechanical or other, including photocopying or information storage, in whole or in part. May not be used to prepare other publications without written permission from the publisher except in the case of brief quotations embodied in critical articles or reviews. For information contact info@earnshawbooks.com

Published in Hong Kong by Earnshaw Books Ltd.

For my Mother
Shulamis 'Shirley' Froloff Hoffmann
A Humble Heroine

Shalama - Hanukkah at the Shanghai Jewish Club - December 1944

Foreword

My first twenty years were spent in New York City. Dinner at a Chinese restaurant was always a treat. Although Mom loved to experiment with different recipes of all ethnicities in the kitchen, she rarely cooked Chinese at home. We frequented a number of Chinese restaurants, but my family especially looked forward to our annual excursion into Manhattan to eat at a Chinese restaurant on 100th Street and Broadway that prepared Peking Duck, which had to be ordered 24 hours in advance. Mom would inevitably engage the young waiters in conversation, asking them where they were from, not content with a response that solely included China. She wanted specifics. In response to the waiters' quizzical looks she would then tell them that she was born in Harbin and lived in Shanghai. She had spent the first twenty four years of her life in China.

In 2021 I had the pleasure of publishing my father's memoir, *Witness to History: From Vienna to Shanghai*. My Dad, Paul Hoffmann, left Vienna, Austria and went to Shanghai, China in 1938 to escape the Holocaust. Dad intended his memoir solely for the family. After the opening of the Shanghai Jewish Refugees Museum in Shanghai in 2007 there was a renewed interest in the Jewish Community who resided in Shanghai. Over the next ten years word spread and continues to generate worldwide interest, about this community: Baghdadi Jews, stateless Russian Jews and Jewish refugees from Central Europe, predominantly from Germany and Austria. The building housing the museum has special significance for my family. It is the former Ohel Moshe Synagogue. I believed that my parents were married in the Ohel

SHALAMA

Moshe on March 5, 1950, as their wedding invitation indicated. While doing the research for this book I discovered this to be incorrect. The Ohel Moshe Synagogue, which is the museum, was built on Ward Road in Hongkew in 1928 by the Russian Ashkenazi community. My parents were married in the New Ohel Moshe Synagogue on Route Tenant de la Tour in the French Concession built in 1941 by the Russian Jewish community that had prospered in Shanghai. Jewish life continued in Shanghai under the communist Regime until 1957. Approximately 500 stateless Russian Jews were stranded there, unable to obtain visas, until a Good Samaritan in the Philippines intervened on their behalf. The synagogues shut down with their departure.

The museum housed at the Ward Road Ohel Moshe has grown considerably since its inception in 2007. Pieces of silverware, wedding gifts to my parents in 1950, are now on display, donated when I visited the museum in 2019. The names of my father, his parents and my aunt and uncle are engraved on the tribute wall in the courtyard of the museum.

I spent two years editing Dad's manuscript, while compiling pictures, letters and documents to enhance and support the text. It truly became a labor of love and it has been very rewarding to see it to completion. Finishing that project left me knowing that I wasn't done. My mother, a stateless Russian Jew, who was born in Harbin, and lived in Shanghai, had a very different story to tell, but left no written record of her family's experience. The basis for this book is a ninety minute oral interview and the stories I was told throughout my lifetime. For this reason, I chose to write this book as historical fiction, combining my mother's story with research, supported by historical documents and photographs. Historical fiction has given me the freedom to imagine the emotions, trauma and voice of my mother and her family. I have done my very best to tell this within actual historical context, so the people and the places are real. Names have only been changed if I had no written record of that person's name. I hope the stories that had not been recorded, and the mysteries of family lost, will serve to intrigue the reader as another unique historical experience is brought to life.

Jean Hoffmann Lewanda
February 2024

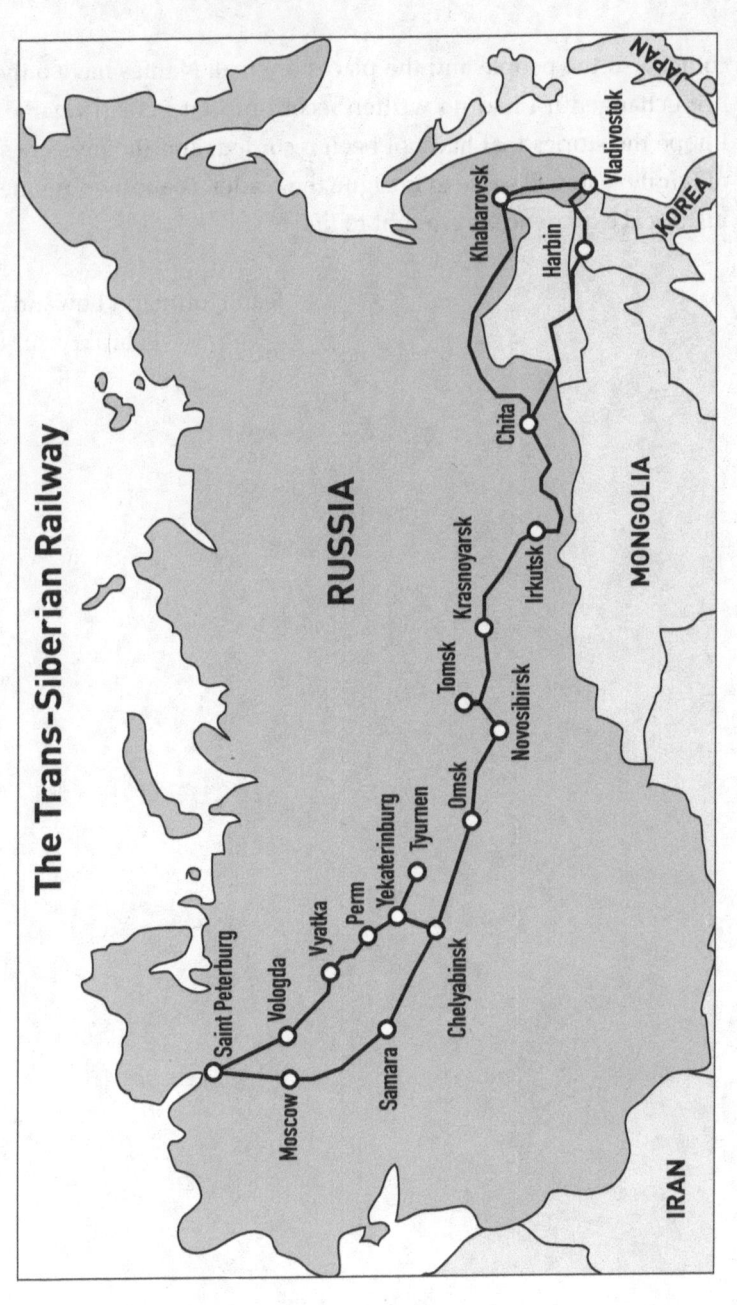

CHAPTER ONE
Reflection
Connecticut 2003

I never really thought I had a story to tell. Or, maybe I did. Always telling stories. Never planned. Never intentionally. Always in the moment, when the stories suddenly came back to me; an unplanned connection between the past and the present.

Perhaps, just maybe, this was because of the stories in my life that were never told, never heard, events never explained, stories that I wished, with all my heart and soul, had been told. My shy, quiet father, who I adored, remained a mystery, dying at age fifty-one, much too young, remaining cloaked in the shadow of secrecy. Who was this handsome man? Yes, he was Papa, but there was something hidden behind his loving countenance, a secret so deep, I wondered if even Mama knew. What was behind this facade that he could not share?

Papa did tell us he hitchhiked for a year, across almost the entire Asian continent, from the small town of Nevel, a shtetl[1] south of St. Petersburg to Harbin, China. Why would someone leave their home to undertake such a long journey, leaving family and friends, all that

---

1   Yiddish for small town.

was familiar? Papa said he didn't want to serve in the Red Army. He said serving in the Red Army meant many years of hunger in places where you could freeze to death. Just a little more than two decades before Papa arrived, Harbin had been a remote Chinese fishing village on the Sungari River in the province of Manchuria in northeastern China, just a little more than 300 miles from Vladivostok. Big changes came to Harbin when China leased the land to build the Chinese Eastern Railway, an extension of the Trans Siberian Railroad, to the Russians to connect Vladivostok to Harbin. Czar Nicholas II promised the Jews freedom from discrimination and educational quotas if they took advantage of the opportunity to help build the railway and settle in China. By the time Papa arrived in 1919, almost twenty years old, Harbin was a bustling European style city, populated by both Russian Orthodox Christians and Jews, living alongside the Chinese. For thirty years Harbin would become a European city, a 'Paris of the East. This was a chance to build a life and family far from the Cossack pogroms and the tyranny of the Red Army.

Was his name really Avram Froloff? My brother and I argued about this again and again, with very little to base our argument on, but we argued nonetheless. Like most siblings, we could make arguments into sport. How was it that our name was Froloff, a generic Russian name, the equivalent of Anglo Smiths? And we are Jewish, which Froloffs typically are not. The scar on Papa's right hand had long healed into a smooth ridge where he severed the tendon between his thumb and pointer finger. It was not unusual for Jewish boys to inflict this injury on themselves in order to avoid serving in the army. If the Russians came looking for him, Papa would be of little use to them because he could no longer fire a gun. And he never spoke of, or even mentioned the names of any of the family he left behind in his shtetl of Nevel. We knew nothing of what their lives were like; only that there were babies at home when he left at nineteen years of age. That's all, nothing more. If we tried to ask Papa questions about his past, he would remind us that we had homework or chores to do, or tell us it was time for bed. As we got older, we saw the discomfort and despair on Papa's face if we persisted. Eventually we stopped asking questions. My quiet, complacent Papa never revealed the fear that must have lived within him; fear that he would be found, fear that those left behind in Nevel would suffer the consequences of his desertion.

If Papa had lived longer, into a time of prosperity and peace, would he have found a moment to tell us his story? He lived his entire life on the edge of poverty and war, too concerned about trying to create a future to reflect on the past.

So I begin...My name is Shalama, a nickname, the name my Russian relatives and friends called me; the name I like best of all the names I have had throughout my life; softer and more affectionate than my legal name, Shulamis, and less bold than my anglicized name, Shirley (chosen when I arrived in Shanghai because Shirley Temple was all the rage). I was named for my uncle Solomon, or Shlomo, as he would have been called in Yiddish, who died by drowning in the river when he was only nineteen years old. None of us ever learned to swim, even though I tried later in life as my husband, Paul, coaxed and encouraged me; even taking adult swim lessons. I watched my children become excellent swimmers, frolicking with Paul, in oceans, rivers and lakes as I sat watching patiently on the shore. My younger brother, named Tuvia for my mother's father, almost drowned when as an engine mechanic serving in the Israeli Defense Force, was shoved off a boat in jest. Although the fear of immersing ourselves in water never left us, we crossed the wide Sungari River multiple times every summer by rowboat when we stayed with our Baba at her dacha[2] on Sun Island. I was never afraid to make this trip; only excited to spend the summer gardening with Baba and visiting with the farm animals. The image that remains in my mind's eye, and brings a smile to my face until this

---

2 Cottage.

day, is the struggle to retrieve the straw sun hat that would blow off my head. Baba would hold me around the waist as I leaned over the edge of the boat. Using an oar, I would try to retrieve the hat before it began floating downstream. More often than not, the next trip across the river to replenish provisions included the purchase of another hat.

So now you know that I am Russian, but born in China. I never set foot on Russian soil until a visit to St.Petersburg, a stop on a cruise through the Baltics, when I was seventy years old. The first twelve years of my life were spent in Harbin, China; way up north, north of North Korea, where it is not unusual for the temperature to dip to -35 degrees Fahrenheit during the long frigid winters. Yet, when summer arrived and the temperature soared into the 80s, my fair freckled skin was often raw and blistered from the sun.

I have told you the very little bit I know about my father's history. I have so much more to tell about my mother's family. Tuvia and Golda came from Novozibkov, a shtetl fourteen miles east of Gomel in the Pale of Settlement, the area established by Catherine the Great in 1791, where Jews were allowed to have permanent residency. Tuvia Egutkin and Golda Riva Estrin had six daughters and one son. Those were the ones that survived infancy. There were twelve pregnancies. Five infant sons spent from minutes to months on this earth, spared hunger and poverty, but deprived of warm family celebrations and so many adventures. Their three oldest daughters, Sonia, Chaya, and Etka, remained behind in Gomel, a city now in Belarus, already married when Tuvia and Golda decided to seek a better life in Harbin. Their younger daughters, Genia, Nehama and Fanya, and son Solomon accompanied them on the long train ride to Vladivostok on the Trans Siberian Railway, and then on to Harbin on the Chinese Eastern Railway. Tuvia succumbed to dysentery shortly after their arrival, leaving Golda to raise her young family on her own. It would be two years later, when carousing on the river with friends, that a row boat would accidentally capsize and Solomon would lose his life. I am the daughter of Fanya, their youngest, destined for a life no one could foresee.

Shalama had been sitting in her living room bathed by the warm afternoon sun, surrounded by dark carved wooden furniture and bright red tapestries of wool and silk that left China with her more than fifty years before. From another room came the strains of La Traviata, Italian opera, where her husband, Paul, also of more than fifty years, listened to his favorite music as he read the New York Times. She awaited the arrival of her nineteen-year-old granddaughter, Cara, home from college on winter break.

Shalama, short in stature, now white-haired, walked with a cane but still with a certain vitality in her step. When the doorbell rang, it took her a moment to rise from her chair, but her round high-cheekboned face and bright brown eyes reflected her eagerness as Cara entered the room. Shalama greeted Cara with a kiss on each cheek and a warm hug. It had been four months since they had seen each other. Long, sometimes endless separations from family had been the norm over Shalama's seventy-five years. To see her grandchildren as often as she did these days was a gift.

"Come in, come in, Cara, mamela! Sit!" Cara switched on her tape recorder. In her soft, gently accented voice Shalama began her story, accompanied by the warm streaming rays of the sun from the western sky.

Chapter Two
Avram
Harbin - 1922

"Fanya! Fanya!" Have you seen him?

"Who?" Fanya's voice sounded bored and tired. She stood over a large cast iron pot in the fenced-in backyard behind the complex of three and four story apartments, on *Bolotnaia Ulitsa*[3] where the Egudkin family lived alongside many other Jewish families. In 1917, just four years earlier, like their neighbors, the Egudkins had fled the violence of the pogroms and the Bolshevik Revolution in Czarist Russia. Fanya had been just twelve years old. This community, predominantly created by White Russians[4], seemed safer and offered more promise. That's not to say that there was no antisemitism. There was. But for a time, before the arrival of the Japanese, there was a relatively peaceful coexistence that allowed some Jewish families to establish themselves and acquire wealth. This was not the case for the Egudkins. Without a father, and no other males in the household to help support them, the four Egudkin women depended on the generosity of

---
3   Bolotnaia Ulitsa — Russian for "Swamp Street".
4   Opponents of the Russian Revolution.

family and the Jewish Community. Golda Riva knew the sooner each one of her daughters married, the better off they all would be.

Fanya, now almost seventeen years old, shivered as she plucked the feathers from a large plump chicken. The bird had been slaughtered earlier in the day as prescribed by the laws of kashrut. According to the Torah, this was the humane way to butcher an animal, quickly severing its throat in one motion so it feels no pain. The *shochet*[5] in Harbin would walk the neighborhood on Friday mornings offering his services. He had performed the ritual act right there in the backyard. Incredibly, this bird hopped off the chopping block, its headless body doing a quick circle of the yard before it fell to the ground.

Fanya's older sister by two years, Genia, stood at the back door of the apartment house on Bolotnaia Ulitsa. She had her shawl wrapped around her head and shoulders as the cold November wind blew the door shut behind her with a loud slam. Layers of woolen clothing were the only defense against the brutal winter cold that arrived in Harbin in October and stayed until March. The resemblance between Fanya and Genia left no doubt that they were sisters. All the women in the family were somewhat *zaftig*[6] and had round high cheek-boned faces surrounded by light brown hair.

"You can't tell me you haven't noticed him," continued Genia. "The young man, Avram! I heard he came from a town near St. Petersburg. He may be the handsomest one yet!" Avram's features were neither Russian nor Jewish. He had soft wavy brown hair with a small, yet masculine nose and well-defined chin. His build was thin, one that any Jewish mother would be pleased to fatten up.

---

5 Individual trained to perform ritual kosher slaughter.
6 Yiddish for 'plump'.

SHALAMA

"Mama has invited him for *Shabbas* dinner tonight. Hurry with the chicken. You know the sun will be setting early. We only have a few hours to finish cooking. The *kugel*[7] is in the oven and the potatoes and carrots have been cooking for the *tzimmes*[8] since last night. We need the chicken for the soup. And do clean yourself up little sister! This dinner is about more than feeding the new arrival in town."

Genia turned and went back into the house to continue preparations for the Sabbath. She had to stand on her tiptoes to reach the unmatched brass candlesticks that sat on the shelf in the sitting room during the week. Genia was always surprised by the heavy weight of the candlesticks in her hands as she carefully lowered them and placed them on the table. No one knew for how many generations these candlesticks were part of every Sabbath and holiday celebration, but Golda Riva had brought them with her on the long train ride from Novozibkov.

Fanya smiled to herself as she dropped the chicken into the pot and began walking back towards the house, clumsily struggling under its weight, now containing the chicken and water drawn from the well. She had to admit she had noticed Avram as she swept the front steps each morning. He passed by the Egudkin apartment as he exited Konnaya Ulitsa 14, a building shared by several Jewish families, on his way to the sewing machine repair shop on Kitaiskaia Ulitsa[9] in the busy center of town. Yitzhak Shmulovich owned the shop and needed a younger pair of hands to help with repairs these days. Fanya had heard Yitzhak's wife, Ida, tell Mama they had taken Avram in as a boarder when they heard that the young man from Nevel had mechanical skills. In exchange for room and board, and a commission on each machine

---
7   A baked casserole made from potatoes or noodles.
8   A stew made from dried fruits and root vegetables.
9   Chinese Street.

he repaired, Avram agreed to work in the shop. He had arrived in Harbin with the clothes on his back and not much else after his year-long journey, a combination of hitchhiking and train rides. Now every mama in the community was wondering if he would make a good match for their young daughter. Avram, although appearing reticent upon introduction, readily accepted all offers for dinner. And he had noticed Fanya, too. He would be twenty-three in March. Now that he had employment and a roof over his head, his mind was free to entertain thoughts of the future.

CHAPTER THREE
Turbulence
Harbin 1924–1932

It would be two years before Fanya and Avram would stand under the *chuppah*, the wedding canopy, in the Main Synagogue on a cold Sunday afternoon in January. Rabbi Aharon Kiselev, Chief Rabbi of Harbin, officiated in Hebrew. Rabbi Kiselev was known to the people who had come from Novozibkov. He had attended yeshiva[10] as a youngster in nearby Gomel. He completed his studies in Minsk at the prestigious Vlojeenskaya Yeshiva. Rabbi Kiselev was not only a man of faith and science, but also an ardent Zionist. In 1913, the Harbin Jewish community organized a selection committee to choose a chief Rabbi. They traveled to Borissov to meet with Rabbi Kiselev, where his personality, oratory skills, and wisdom impressed the committee. In September of that year he became the Chief Rabbi of Harbin.

The morning of the wedding Fanya awoke before the rooster crowed. It was January and it was Harbin. Although the sun would be up soon, the day would be short. The sun would set

---
10 Traditional Jewish educational institution focused on the study of rabbinic literature.

early that winter day. The outdoor temperature was well below zero and the three brightly colored duck down comforters were pulled up over her head to keep out the morning chill. Today was the day she would marry Avram. Avram, handsome and quiet, but what did she really know about him? For the last several months, since Avram had stated his intentions, after a long day's work he had been having dinner with Fanya and Mama. He spoke of the day's events; who came to the store, how many machines were fixed, the latest street violence perpetrated by the Russian gangs. Fanya begged him to tell more about his family and where he came from. Somehow he always avoided revealing any more about his family than he had already told them. When asked about where he came from, quickly the focus of the conversation shifted to the magnificence of St. Petersburg; the ornate buildings that shone like gold in the sunlight, the wide thoroughfares graced by tall trees along the Neva River that cast cooling shadows in the warmer months, but became stark statues during the bitter cold of winter. There were the richly dressed wealthy in their fur coats as they strolled the Nevsky Prospekt, St. Petersburg's main boulevard. A few blocks away these affluent citizens, were starkly contrasted to, and vastly out-numbered by the peasantry in worn wool coats, some begging for food. Avram had only been to St. Petersburg once, on his way to Harbin. There had been great hope for the Jewish people after the February 1917 Revolution. All Jews were allowed to live in the city, not only the 'useful Jews', the ones the Czars needed: the financiers, doctors, lawyers, industrialists and engineers who would help them grow their power. Nine months later the Bolshevik Revolution again threatened the rights and property of Jews. Joseph Trumpeldor[11], the most decorated

---

11 Joseph Trumpeldor was the hero and role model for the Betar Movement, a Revisionist Zionist Youth Movement, which was active in Harbin, Tientsin, and Shanghai. Betar is an acronym Brit Trumpeldor, which translates to *The Covenant of Trumpeldor*.

Jewish soldier in Russia, commanded a self-defense unit, to protect the Jews of St. Petersburg. Avram sensed that Trumpeldor knew Russia would never be a homeland for the Jews. While Avram began his journey across the Asian continent, Trumpeldor was on his way to Palestine[12].

Before dawn on the day he left Nevel, Avram joined his neighbor, Nacham, on the winding dirt road leading out of town. Nacham was pulling a dray towards the outskirts of town, where he would collect the cans of milk to deliver to the residents of the Nevel. When they reached the end of the fence that surrounded the pasture where the cows grazed, Nacham embraced Avram and wished him a safe journey.

"You are a brave young man," said Nachum. "The Far East, Harbin! China! Such a great distance! So strange! Who knows what your future holds? But I will pray for you. Go with God."

This is all Fanya knew about her husband to be. But, none of this mattered this frigid Harbin morning. Fanya was the youngest of her six sisters and the last to be married. Her husband would be the handsomest of all the men in the family! And Avram was so kind, in his own quiet way. Fanya was almost twenty years old. She knew it was time to start a family. Somehow she knew in her heart that Avram would make a good husband.

Fanya's family was well represented at the wedding: her mother, two of her older sisters, Nehama and Genia, their husbands, a few young nieces and nephews, several aunts, uncles and cousins, as well as friends and acquaintances. Not a single member of Avram's family was present. Did his family even know that he was taking a bride that day? Everyone watched as Fanya circled her groom seven times while the *chazzan*[13] chanted

---

[12] Trumpeldor died defending Jewish farming villages in the Upper Galilee in 1920. Kiryat Shmona, City of Eight, is named for Trumpeldor and the seven others who died in the Battle of Tel Hai.

[13] Cantor.

the seven blessings for a long and fruitful life. After a generous meal of borsch, kugel, meat, fish, *kreplach*[14], *blini*[15] and cakes, the bride and groom retired to what would be their room in Golda's small apartment. Later that year their first child, a daughter, Manya, would arrive. Three years later I would join the family, and three years after me came my brother, Tuvia, whom we called Teva.

Life was simple in Harbin for my first seven years, which were spent at home with family. Formal schooling did not start until age seven, so we children were free to play. Occasionally, we were asked to run an errand, or help with the chores that suited our age and size, but mostly we entertained each other. We spent our time with our cousins and neighbors, outdoors when the weather allowed.

The highlight of the summer months was staying with Baba in the small wooden *dacha* on Sun Island. It was just two rooms and the bath house was a separate small structure out back. In late April, sometime after Pesach, I would begin helping Baba pack our clothing and provisions. Papa would load the heavy boxes onto a wooden wagon he had borrowed from a neighbor and take us down to the river bank. There we would meet our cousin, Big Tolia, Nehama's only child, a tall strapping young man. Big Tolia was the proud owner of a row boat that his father, Grisha, had purchased from a Chinese fisherman. Big Tolia's boat would take us and other family members back and forth across the river throughout the summer. It would take three or four trips to transport all we needed to stay on the island. There were the cooking pots, some warm clothing for the cooler nights, and of course, the samovar to make *chai*, tea. Nehama and Genia each had their own dacha for their families, but we would stay

---

14 Dumplings.
15 Crepe-like pancakes.

with Baba. I was the only one that stayed the entire summer. Mama would spend a few days at a time with Manya and Teva, and Papa would come for a day or two when work would allow. It was my very special time with Baba. We had our own garden. At the end of the summer I loved harvesting the peanuts and potatoes. There we were, Baba and me, barefoot, digging away, feeling around in the dirt with our hands, carefully searching for buried treasure. By the time we were done for the day, our faces were streaked with grimy sweat and our hands and feet were caked with mud. We would go down to the river bank and submerge ourselves up to our waists, clothes and all. Baba would command me to close my eyes, as she poured bucket after bucket of icy cold water over my head to get the dirt out of my hair. "Shalaminka, you look like a river rat," she would say, and then pull me close to her to warm me up as we walked back to the dacha. After a long day of gardening, I struggled to keep my eyes open through dinner.

Some days Baba would send me to the nearby farmer for eggs and sunflower oil. She never even needed to ask when it was time to go to the farm. At breakfast, Baba would say, "I'm thinking of making blini for lunch today." I would quickly chime in, "And to make blini, you need eggs and oil!" Baba knew not to expect me back for several hours when I went to visit the farm. After wishing the Chinese farmer *dobre utra*, good morning in Russian, he would hand me a bucket with grain. The chickens, ducks, and geese would quickly gather around me as I tossed them their breakfast. The farmer always had a carrot saved for me to feed his pony. No visit was complete without taking the pony for a ride around the small pasture. On the way home, using a sharp thorn, I would poke a small hole in one of the eggs in the basket I carried over my shoulder and suck its contents right from the shell. The sunflower oil was in a quart size metal canister. I would stop and loosen the top to sip the rich tasty oil as I walked the narrow unpaved path back to the dacha.

The summer months are the rainiest months of the year in Northern China. When we arrived on Sun Island in June of 1932 we were not surprised rain fell every few days. Then July came, and the rains became steadier and more frequent. Baba stood by the window and watched as the waters of the mighty Sungari River rose higher and higher. One morning, during the third week in July, she looked at me and said, "It is time to go home."

"But, Baba, we can't leave! The potatoes and peanuts are nowhere near ready!"

"I know, I know," Baba's saddened voice responded. "But look at the river. Everyday it rises higher and it has been raining every day for five days now. If the river gets much higher, I am afraid Tolia's small boat will be no match for the rushing current. Go next door to Aunt Nehama's and tell Tolia to get the boat ready. I think it is time for us all to leave." No one ever questioned Baba's quiet intuitive wisdom. The packing for the exodus from Sun Island began.

It took the entire day and several trips to get all of us and our belongings back to our homes in the city. The streets of Harbin were already becoming small rivers and the Chinese people who lived in the lower end of town began to seek higher ground. Our summer of fun and adventure was now one of confinement and fear. There was no going outdoors as we watched the water in the streets rise. We leaned on the windowsill, gazing out for hours with little else to do. Our white kitten, Koshky, a gift from the farmer on Sun Island, perched herself on the windowsill between Teva and I. After lunch, I would be the only one watching for the occasional burst of activity, as both Teva and Koshky would be taking their afternoon naps. The shops on Kitaiskaia Ulitsa were forced to shut their doors as the water began to seep in.

SHALAMA

Soon there were row boats navigating the streets, bringing what could be salvaged to the upper end of town. As more and more homes became submerged, the boats would be carrying people and their belongings away from the rising waters. Many of those who tried to stay, mostly the Chinese, not only lost their homes but lost their lives. The Jewish community fared better. Word spread that water must be boiled before drinking and all fruits and vegetables must be peeled and cooked before eating to avoid cholera, which was spreading rapidly. Jewish doctors boarded row boats to visit the sick. The young men and women of Betar, the Zionst youth organization founded in 1923, corralled their members, first to fill sandbags in an attempt to stop the rising waters, then to rescue the elderly and bring them to the synagogue, welfare kitchen, school or hospital. With that mission accomplished the Betarim began delivering bread and water to isolated families, paddling around the neighborhood calling out to check on the status of each family.

It was a lonely summer. All I remember after we returned to Harbin city was the endless waiting. Waiting for the rain to stop, waiting for Papa to come home when he dared to venture out, and waiting to eat. The supply of food for a family of six began to dwindle quickly, especially because it was summer and we were used to obtaining all our food fresh every day from the farmers selling their products from their kiosks in the bazaar. If we were still on Sun Island, I would be sitting on the banks of the Sungari with a string and hook. Baba had taught me to ball up a piece of bread, place it on a hook and drop the string in the water. In no time at all, I would catch several small, shiny black fish that I would bring back to the dacha in the bucket Baba had given me. That night for dinner we would have delicious fish, pan fried in the aromatic sunflower oil I had gotten from the farmer earlier in the day. Nothing tasted better. Now as the rain fell for close to four weeks and the streets became impassable, we couldn't even go into town to purchase food in the shops. Shpunt Delicatessen, which my friend Musia's papa owned, was inundated with water and was unsalvageable. I wouldn't see Musia again for several years. Rather than rebuild, her family left for Shanghai to start over, a path many families would take in the coming months and years. After four weeks the water finally receded. Harbin was an unrecognizable mess. Not only had many businesses been destroyed, so had the harvest from all the surrounding regions and very little food was being brought into the city by the Chinese farmers. Waiting to eat was going to be something we would have to get used to for the months to come.

The winter of 1932 brought changes. Mama and Papa stopped sending us with our older cousins to pick up bread and milk on Kitaiskaia Ulitsa. We were told to stay in our courtyard. The Japanese had entered Harbin. They had begun their takeover of Manchuria in 1931. It was now Manchukuo, a puppet state of the Empire of Japan. Papa, Manya and I stood holding hands as we watched from the rooftop of the repair shop as Chinese General Ting-Chao tried to stave off the Japanese forces entering Harbin in the sub-zero temperatures. The White Russian and Japanese members of the community cheered as they watched the Chinese forces crumble right in front of the Russian offices of the Chinese Eastern Railway. We, stateless Russian Jews, watched in silence, never knowing what our fate would be as a new ruling power took hold. The next day, the Japanese soldiers posted notices that Harbin was under martial law and that the inhabitants of the city would not be harmed. But martial law did not prevent the anarchy and chaos that followed.

For the members of our family there was little change. Our cousin, Tolia Bluestein, Nehama's son, was the oldest boy, so if we needed anything in town, he would take Tolia Singaus, Aunt

Genia's son, the next oldest boy, with him. We called him Little Tolia, not because he was small, just younger than Big Tolia, so as not to confuse them. All the boys carried some form of our deceased grandfather's name in his memory.

You'd think because we were poor we would have more trouble than our more affluent neighbors, but it was just the opposite. Those members of the community who were of means had far more to worry about. The Japanese aligned themselves with the antisemitic Russian gangs and their notorious leader, Konstantin Rodzaevsky, head of the RFP, the Russian Fascist Party, and his lieutenant, Martinoff. A number of prominent members of the Harbin Jewish community were kidnapped and held for ransom. Some of these kidnappings ended tragically in death. Rodzaevsky was able to convince the Japanese that his actions were motivated not by antisemitism or greed, but by an anti-communist agenda, which the Japanese supported, and the worst perpetrators literally got away with murder. As long as we stayed in our neighborhood, on the poor side of town, we felt safe.

CHAPTER FOUR
Trauma
Harbin 1932–1933

The Jewish Free Soup Kitchen at the Social Aid Committee building in town was kept busy all that fall and winter. The Harbin Flood Refugee Committee was established to help residents recover from the devastation. Although our apartment had survived the destruction brought by the rising and then slowly receding water, we were not the only ones whose pantries were empty and we joined other members of the community in the line that formed on Friday mornings to ensure we had food for the Sabbath. When spring arrived, Mama donned a white head scarf and apron and joined others under a tarp to bake matzah for Passover. Volunteering her time guaranteed us a portion of the freshly baked matzah at no cost. We would have enough matzah to take us through the eight day observance.

Passover was my favorite holiday. Sometimes, one of the Seders, the ritual Passover meal, would fall on my birthday, March 31. (We celebrated two Seders, like all Jews in the Diaspora, to ensure that we were observing within the prescribed time in the Holy Land.)

SHALAMA

Life cycle events in our community were celebrated on the lunar Jewish calendar, which meant the actual date varied from year to year. In 1933, April 10 was the first Seder night and I was five years old. Baba, Aunt Genia, Aunt Nehama and Mama would begin preparations several weeks before. They cleaned and scrubbed every nook and cranny of their houses. The brass candlesticks were polished until they reflected the candle light. We could not afford a separate set of Passover dishes and cookware so all the tableware was boiled in big kettles in the yard. All the *chametz*[16] was consumed the day before the start of the holiday. We children would run around the yard hoping that a biscuit or two would end up in our hands as we chased after each other in a game of tag. By Erev Pesach, the evening before the first Seder, when all the papas had arrived home, we watched the ritual burning of the very last piece of leavened bread. You can be sure it was just a tiny piece, just enough to fulfill the *mitzvah*.[17] Food was just too scarce to let more than necessary be used for anything other than feeding our families.

Our Seders went long into the night, retelling the Exodus from Egypt, the story that started it all. After all, what were Jews doing in China? Weren't we still on our 2,000 year journey to reclaim our homeland? We repeated at each Seder "Next year in Jerusalem." Forty years in the desert, forty years in China. Diaspora defined us.

We all gathered at Aunt Genia's home since she had the largest apartment. Uncle Singaus, whom I always addressed by his last name, led the Seder. We prayed, we ate, we prayed some more and then we ate some more. After dinner the singing started with the papas trading shots of vodka. The traditional songs, Dayenu, *It Would Have Been Enough,* and Had Gadya, *One*

---

16   Any food product made from grain and not considered Kosher for Passover.
17   A commandment to fulfill a religious duty.

Little Goat, were punctuated by raucous laughter. The enormous meal, the revelry, and the wine we clandestinely sipped from each of the four cups of wine our parents drank as part of the ritual meal, found us by the end of the evening under the table where we had fallen asleep. Papa would gently pull Manya, who was now eight years old, and me out from under the table and carry us home to bed.

The summer seemed uneventful compared to the events of the previous year; no floods or Japanese invasions. Baba's apartment had become too small for our family of five so the big excitement was the warm August Sunday when we moved to our own three-room apartment on Bolotnaia Ulitsa, two blocks closer to the unpaved end of the street. Uncle Singaus, Little Tolia, Uncle Grisha and Big Tolia were all there to load up the wagons with the beds, pots and pans, clothing, and the few pieces of furniture that Baba could spare. Aunt Genia and Uncle Singaus provided us with a table and five chairs. Aunt Nehama and Uncle Grisha had an extra rug and an old overstuffed upholstered chair. When we arrived at the apartment there was a footstool and two chests of drawers waiting at the front door, used but in good condition, gifts from our neighbors who knew we wouldn't have enough to furnish our new home.

The apartment was small, only three rooms. A bedroom for Mama and Papa, a bedroom for us children, and a larger room that served as a living room and dining room with a cast iron stove in the corner. There was no indoor plumbing. We children were allowed to use a chamber pot under the bed at night rather than brave the frigid cold. Our parents were not so lucky and had to use the outhouse.

We had electricity, but it was temperamental. Sometimes we had to slam the door to turn on the lights. One day, I hadn't noticed that Koshsky was warming herself in the doorway as the afternoon sun was setting. The front room was beginning to get dark. With all my might, I slammed the door. The kitten flew across the room and landed motionless in the middle of the faded, red flowered rug that Aunt Nehama had given us, which covered the planks of the rough-hewn floor. I cradled Koshsky in my arms as tears streamed down my face. Papa had just arrived home from work. He had heard the door slam even before he had entered the house, so it didn't take long to figure out what happened. The door must have snapped the poor thing's neck. Papa went back to the repair shop and returned with a wooden box. Mama went through her basket of sewing scraps and we lined the box with the softest cloth we could find, a small piece of light blue silk leftover from a blouse Baba had made for Manya for the Hannukah celebration the year before, and gently placed Koshky in the wooden box. The next day we buried her in the courtyard of the apartment building. We covered the tiny grave with leaves. Until snow covered her grave, I visited Koshky everyday, replacing the leaves that had blown away overnight and asking Koshky's forgiveness for slamming the door so terribly hard.

    Manya and I were inseparable, except for the time she was in school. She had started at the primary Jewish School the previous fall. I watched as she donned her dark blue school uniform each morning, wishing I could go with her. Mama would part her long brown tresses in the middle of her scalp and form two braids, one over the front of each shoulder. After breakfast, Papa walked with Manya down the unpaved portion of street leading into town. He would walk with her until they met up with our older cousins and they would all walk to school together while Papa went off to the sewing machine repair shop.

    I sat on the front stoop of our apartment on Bolotnaia Ulitsa, eagerly awaiting Manya each afternoon when she returned from school. She would relate all that happened throughout the day. I loved when she taught me the songs she had learned, both in Russian and Hebrew. As we lay in bed each night she would tell me the story that her teacher had read to the class that day. Mama promised me each morning that soon I would be able to go to school with Manya, but this would never be.

One day in early December, our cousin, Little Tolia, came running into the shop where Papa worked.

"Uncle Avram! Uncle Avram! Come quickly! Manya is sick! Her teacher sent me to get you!"

"Tolia, what do you mean Manya is sick? It is only one o'clock in the afternoon and I have several more machines to fix before I leave for the day." Papa did not disguise the frustration in his voice. Every repaired sewing machine meant a few more Manchukuo yuan and another meal or two for the family.

"Really, Uncle Avram. She said her head hurt, and then her stomach hurt, and then she threw up in the back of the classroom."

Papa grabbed his hat and coat and quickly followed Tolia the four blocks back to the school. When they arrived, Manya was lying on a bench in the hallway outside her classroom, her brown woolen coat draped over her. Her face was ashen, drained of all color and she whispered, "I am so sorry, Papa. I told them it was too early for you to leave work." Papa said nothing and scooped her up in his arms and ran with her to the outpatient clinic at the Jewish Hospital a few blocks from the school. Dr. Kaufman met them in the foyer and immediately took them into an examining room. Papa was well acquainted with Dr. Kaufman since he was a leader of the Zionist Organization of Harbin, whose meetings Papa regularly attended, and the respected head of our Jewish Community. Manya was running a high fever and had an angry red rash all over her torso.

"Avram, how long has she been like this?"

"Just today," Avram answered. She may have been a little tired and not as hungry as usual for the past few days, but she loves school and is always eager to go. She was up and ready to leave before I was this morning."

Dr. Kaufman gave Papa a bottle of quinine. "Take Manya home. Give her the quinine morning and night, and try to get her to drink. And pray. She has typhoid fever. She must have eaten some contaminated food and there is not much else we can do but let the disease run its course. It is now in God's hands."

Papa picked up Manya's limp little body. Dr. Kaufman's face revealed more than he intended as he gently draped Manya's coat over her. Papa held his little girl close to his chest. This would be one of the many life-threatening diseases Dr. Kaufman would see that winter. He asked himself, "What gave people the courage to make this strange frigid isolated place their home?" He felt helpless that there was nothing more that he could do.

Papa walked the several blocks to their home, with his arms tightly wrapped around his oldest child, keeping her warm, vowing nothing would take her from him.

Mama was standing on the front stoop waiting with Aunt Genia by her side, when they arrived. Tolia, instead of returning to his class, had run home to share the news about Manya. Genia ran to her baby sister's home, knowing Fanya would need her support. When Genia saw Manya in Papa's arms it took all her strength not to cry out at the sight of her niece's pale face and limp limbs. The color immediately drained from Mama's face.

"*Gott im himmel!*"[18] Mama cried out. She took Manya from Papa's arms and quickly took her into the apartment, out of the chill of the afternoon.

"Shalama! Teva! Put on your coats, hats, and boots. You will

---

18 God in Heaven in Yiddish.

stay at my house tonight."

"But Aunt Genia, we haven't had dinner yet. And it is so cold out! I want to stay here with Mama and Papa. Manya! Manya! What is wrong? Why isn't she answering me?" I looked from Mama to Papa. I saw the tears in Mama's eyes. Now there were tears in my eyes, too.

The next morning, Papa came to Aunt Genia's apartment. He kissed Teva and me, each on the forehead. He told Genia he was going to the shop, but would come home at lunch time. He said not much had changed overnight and turned and walked into town.

Three weeks later, on December 29, 1933, Manya was gone. Mama said that maybe it was better that *HaShem*[19] had taken her.

---

19 Hebrew name for God. The literal translation is "The Name". Observant Jews refer to God in this way as not to say the name of God in daily conversation.

CHAPTER FIVE
Memory
Connecticut 2003

"Amma, I didn't know you had a sister. You told me so many stories, but a sister? How could you not tell me about your sister?" Cara asked in disbelief.

"I guess I buried many of my memories of Manya all these years; and I was so young, there really is not much to tell. Painful memories are often left unspoken. Why live in the past if it causes pain? I never saw Manya again after she came home from school that day. Typhoid fever can be contagious, or at least that's what they thought back then, and Teva and I did not return home until after the New Year. Manya died on a Friday night and in the Jewish tradition burials could not take place on the Sabbath. She was buried that Sunday. My parents did not think young children should be taken to the cemetery so we stayed at Genia's house with our cousin Luba, Tolia's sister, who was eleven years old, which seemed very old to me at the time. Manya was laid to rest with our grandfather, Tuvia. I finally saw Grandfather's headstone before we left Harbin for Shanghai in 1940. It was taller than Papa. We all went to the cemetery to say our goodbyes. I heard that after the communist takeover of China, the Chinese peasants used the *headstones from the Jewish cemetery to build roads and stonewalls. We found out too late that if we had sent fifty dollars in 1958 to the Harbin government, they would have moved the headstone to the Foreigners Cemetery on the outskirts of the city.*

Before we could come home, the neighbors came and scrubbed the apartment from floor to ceiling. Aunt Genia brought us home to sit Shiva[20] with Mama and Papa. Mama was never the same after Manya's death. There was a melancholy and helplessness about her. Her tears flowed for weeks. All Baba's efforts to comfort her were in vain. If anyone knew what it meant to lose a child, it was Baba, but this made little difference to Mama. At times she would wail uncontrollably, asking what she had done for HaShem to punish her by taking her child. Sometimes, Teva or I would sit in her lap and she would rock back and forth, whispering, "pachimu, pachimu[21]" for what seemed like hours. Now I was the big sister. Now Teva was my responsibility, or so I thought. It was my job to make sure Mama did not suffer any more. Manya's death changed me, too. I didn't know it then, but I was learning what it meant to be strong and self-reliant. In many ways, Manya's death may have determined how I was going to face challenges throughout my life. Maybe because Mama seemed so helpless, I became a tough kid."

---

20 Seven day mourning period.
21 Russian - 'why?'.

CHAPTER SIX
School
Harbin 1935-1938

The day finally arrived! I was seven years old and I could go to school. As the sun came up on that crisp fall morning, I smoothed the wrinkles of my navy blue school uniform, which Mama had carefully laid out on the bed next to mine, the bed that had been Manya's. Mama braided my hair over my shoulders, just as she did Manya's, and went to make breakfast for Papa, Teva and me. I could hardly take a bite of my brown bread spread with schmaltz, the bright yellow fat that rose to the top of the chicken soup as it cooled. Mama would skim the fat off the soup, mix in a little salt and we ate it like butter. On any other day, I would be begging for more, but today the butterflies in my stomach took up all the space that was meant for food. We stepped outside and our neighbor, Boris Poldolsky, who owned the photography studio on Kitaiskaia Ulitsa, was there waiting to photograph me. I stood proudly in front of the house, showing off my school uniform. He took pictures of me with Mama, then Papa, and then of the three of us. I gave Mama a huge hug, Teva a quick one, and Papa and I were on our way.

The Harbin Jewish School was a two-story brick building. There was a long curving staircase when you entered through the massive wooden double-doors. The older students climbed the winding staircase, some running, taking two steps at a time, while the younger students meandered down the hallway to their classrooms on the first floor. My friend Stasia, who was one year older than me, took my hand and I followed her to the first classroom. She said, "This is the room for the Form One. See you at recess," as she let go of my hand and crossed the hall to the room for Form Two students.

I loved school even more than I thought possible. We were taught in Russian, but we also learned Hebrew and Japanese. Why Japanese? Because we were still under Japanese occupation; the occupation that started in 1932 didn't end until 1945 when the Japanese were finally defeated in World War II. One of the stranger circumstances of my life, and one that I regret, is that I lived the first twenty-four years of my life in China, and except for a few words, I never learned Chinese. Maybe this was because Harbin never really felt very Chinese with the overwhelming influence of the Russians and the Japanese. You might say we lived in China, but we did not live with the Chinese people. I think our community saw China as a haven, or a stop-over, a temporary home until we could find a real home. A Jewish homeland was still a dream, but a goal for many, nonetheless.

My favorite part of school were the plays and skits we put on for the Jewish holidays. We learned songs and dances for Sukkot and Simchat Torah. And then of course there were the 'dramatic' roles. That first year I was a candle in the menorah for Hanukkah and a *Hamantaschen*[22] for Purim. The students upstairs got the coveted lead roles, portraying Judah Maccabee, Eleazar, John,

---

22　Triangular filled pastry in the shape of Haman's hat.

Simon, Jonathan and Mattathias for Hanukkah and Mordecai, Esther, Ahasuerus, Vashti and Haman for Purim. Purim was the holiday where everyone participated when the Megillah, the Book of Esther, was read aloud from a single scroll kept in a silver engraved case. Every time the name of Haman, the villainous vizier of King Ahashaerus, or his sons, was mentioned, we would spin our groggers[23], holler, and stamp our feet to drown out the names of these evil enemies of the Jewish people.

There was reading, writing and mathematics to challenge us everyday. We had a young male teacher, I think his name was Mr. Yankelovich. He had been to America, where he said he made money washing windows. We quickly discovered if we asked him to tell us about America, we would escape from the far less exciting academic drills that filled our days. Almost every afternoon, as the classroom light was dimming, as the winter sun began to set, someone would raise their hand and say "Mr. Yankelovich, tell us about America." Or, "Is it true that there is a building in New York City that touches the sky?" "Does the sun really shine everyday in California?" Before we, and Mr. Yankelovich, knew it, the dismissal bell rang, and whatever lesson we had not completed would have to wait until the next day. It wasn't such a bad thing. We were learning about America, that mystical place that many in our distant corner of the world still believed had streets that were paved with gold.

Three years later, it was my turn to lead Teva to the First Form classroom. He was a shy, quiet child, who Mama seemed to baby even more since Manya's passing. Tears ran down her cheeks as we once again posed for our first day of school pictures. Instead of standing up straight and proudly showing off his navy blue school uniform with the shiny buttons and smart looking cap,

---

[23] Noise makers.

Teva held Mama's hand and leaned in against her, as if he could hide behind her and not be noticed. When the photographer was done taking our pictures I wedged my fingers between his and Mama's hand, gave Mama a kiss on the cheek and said, *"Tbl khoroshor soldat!" Be a good soldier!"* I wanted both Teva and Mama to be brave.

By this time, the doors of the Harbin Jewish School did not seem quite so massive and it was my friends and I who ran up the curved staircase two steps at a time. It didn't take long for the other children to realize that Teva was an easy target, not one who was going to stand up for himself when confronted. So I assumed the job. One day at recess, I came out onto the play yard with my friends and I heard some of the older boys calling Teva *'soplyak', big baby*. For some reason, I immediately decided this situation would not be rectified by a mere exchange of words. I hauled off and punched a tall dark haired boy in the stomach. I think I surprised him, but he did not think diplomacy was in order either, and retaliated with a punch to the nose. Not only was I a bloody mess, my nose was broken! Now I had a reputation that I maintained throughout my school career in Harbin. My friends knew that they could depend on me to stand up for them and neither Teva, nor any of my friends, were ever again the victims of the bullies on the play yard.

The time after recess was the highlight of the day. Even in the coldest weather we would spend some time outdoors. I wore a mask outdoors, as did many of the other children. I suffered a deep, dry cough for most of the winter. By this time Tolia Bluestein, my oldest cousin, had been trained as a nurse. He would come to our house in the evening as I was getting ready for bed to do 'cupping therapy'. I would lie on my belly and he would apply heated cups to my back that left large red splotches on my skin that became blue bruises over time. I felt such relief as the cough would ease sufficiently so I could fall asleep.

Oh yes, the best time of day...as we came into the hallway outside our classroom, we would shed our coats, scarves, hats, masks and gloves. Then we jockeyed for a spot on the floor closest to the charcoal stove. Even the boys did not hesitate to lean on the shoulders and laps of friends in an effort to share body heat. And then the magic began! Mr. Yankelovich, who had stayed with us through the grades, did not think us too young to hear the marvelous stories and poems of the great Alexander Sergeevich Pushkin. The very first poem he read to us was The Golden Cockerel from Pushkin's fairy tales. Mr. Yankelovich had a deep mellow voice and within moments we were no longer in our small classroom in the extreme cold of Northern China, but in the kingdom of the greedy Czar Dadon, whom at first we admired for wanting to bring peace to his kingdom, but then reviled as we realized his deep-seeded greed. At the close of each story, Mr. Yankelovich would leave us to ponder one of Pushkin's famous quotes. "I lived to bury my desires, and see my dreams corrode with rust. Now all that's left is fruitless fires, that burn my empty heart to dust." We were still too young to grasp the full meaning of these passages, but the music and the rhyme of the language stayed with us and soon we were able to recite these lines by heart.

CHAPTER SEVEN
Change
Harbin 1938–1940

We didn't know it yet, but the world was changing. For now, so removed were we, our lives went on as always: family, school, religious celebrations. Even the most creative of imaginations would struggle to predict what would happen next.

It was around this time, when I was about ten years old, that I became aware of Betar, the Zionist youth organization. Papa continued to be involved with the General Zionists of Harbin. He came home with stories of the Land of Milk and Honey, where the weather was always warm and dates and olives grew on the trees. Rabbi Kiselev's strong support of the Zionist cause fueled the intense interest of the Harbin Jewish Community in return to the Promised Land. He took every opportunity to preach of the importance of the Jewish people reclaiming their homeland. Rabbi Kiselev said we had preserved our Hebrew language, kept it alive through prayer, for more than 2,000 years. We were a people that created and kept our own religion and identity. Our homeland was in British-ruled Palestine, and it was our right to return there.

SHALAMA

Papa said it was important to know you were a Jew. He said it was important to be able to defend yourself. Papa said that one day, we would have a country of our own. One day, there would be a place where Jews wouldn't have to worry about pogroms and antisemitism, in a place where we spoke our own language. We were going to return to the land of our ancestors, a place where we would never have to hide who we were. We would be proud hardworking Jews building a homeland.

Papa began taking Teva and me to sporting events to watch strong, brave Jews compete proudly. The Harbin Betarim excelled at track and field, ping pong and individual sports, such as archery. There were intercity tournaments with the Betarim from Tientsin and Shanghai as well as the fiercely competitive Maccabi, another Zionist youth organization. We were always there to cheer on our friends and classmates on the Harbin team, especially our track star Yaacov Liberman, a handsome young man three years older than me. Yaacov had been to school in Shanghai, but always returned to Harbin in the summer to compete for the Harbin Betarim. When Yaacov was not competing, he was leading us in cheers. He was at the front of every parade. His enthusiasm and charisma convinced us that our future would be in a free Jewish state.

We met other youngsters like us and quickly began to enjoy the camaraderie. I was not athletic, but learned to play volleyball and ping pong, holding the paddle upside down with the handle braced between the pointer and middle finger like the Chinese do. I made friends for life and my life became one that was defined by the principles I learned as a Betari: Stand-up for what you believe. Be ready to defend what is right. I donned my blue military-style Betar uniform and neckerchief proudly. I marched in parades. I carried a rifle in those parades, and I eventually learned to fire it. We set our sights on Palestine, the future State of Israel, and knew that we would be its defenders when the time came.

It wasn't long before we began to hear about a man named Adolph Hitler and how Germany had invaded Austria, Czechoslovkia and Poland. We heard about Jews leaving Europe. Some arrived in Harbin, but most went to Shanghai. Whatever was happening in the world, began to affect us in Harbin. Our bustling European-style city, a city that had experienced miraculous growth and prosperity in the last thirty years, was now suffering under the Japanese occupation. Papa was getting less and less work. Sometimes he disappeared for days at a time. He never said where he was going, but when he came back he always was able to hand Mama some money. She would go into town and come back with meat, fish, bread and vegetables. We would eat well for at least a few days, until what she bought was consumed and then Papa would be gone again.

One early morning, I watched from the window as Papa prepared to leave on one of his 'trips'. I saw a man, in a long dark coat and fur-skinned hat whom I assumed was Russian, drive a black car into the alley between our apartments. He stepped out of the car and opened the trunk. He lifted out an inner tube of a bicycle tire that appeared to be inflated, but also appeared to be very heavy. Papa approached the man and lifted his shirt. The man helped secure the heavy inner tube around Papa's waist. Papa tucked his shirt back into his pants, buttoned his overcoat and began walking down the street. At the next corner, he met another man driving a wagon. The man reached out his hand to help Papa as he strained to climb onto the bench seat of the wagon. I watched until I could no longer see them. Again, Papa was gone for two days and when he returned he handed Mama money to buy food. When we asked Papa where he went and where the money came from, he would reply, "Are you enjoying your dinner?" When we answered "Yes, of course!" he would say "Then thank HaShem for delivering the food and your Mama for preparing it so well." The conversation always ended there.

It was Shabbas when Papa returned from that trip and after dinner, while Mama, Aunt Genia, and Baba cleared the table, Uncle Singaus and Papa had a bottle of vodka between them. I sat in an overstuffed armchair near the wall cuddling my calico cat, Shayna, in my lap. Shayna had been with us since the winter after Koshky died. I tried to look disinterested as I stroked Shayna, struggling to pick up bits of their conversation. After the third shot of vodka, they seemed to forget I was there and made little attempt to speak quietly.

I heard Uncle Singaus say, "Avram, you know what you're doing is very dangerous. Why risk it?"

"The money is too good to pass up," said Papa. "The Japanese need the mercury I'm carrying for their war effort against the Chinese and they can't get it without going through the Russians. Smuggling on the black market is very lucrative. Until we can figure something else out, it's putting food on the table."

Solomon Singaus was a furrier. When he first arrived in Harbin he found work unloading piles of pelts that Russian, Chinese and Japanese fur traders brought from Mongolia and deposited on the banks of the Sungari. Soon Uncle Singaus was working in a fur store, learning from the Chinese workers how to clean and prepare the pelts for the tailors who created the most beautiful luxurious warm coats. The coats were made from ermine, sable, rabbit and bear. There were collars made from beaver, fox, seal and squirrel that were added to cloth coats. There were fancy Russian-style hats for both men and women. He was now a portly, well-dressed balding man approaching middle age. As opposed to Papa who was shy and reserved, he was an outgoing, outspoken and an initiator. Uncle Singaus did not wait to see what would happen next. He made it happen.

One cold Sunday afternoon in November, Uncle Singaus burst into our sitting room. He had a bad habit of never knocking. Papa, who was reading his newspaper as usual, without turning his head, said *'Dobre Dehn, Shlomo. Kak delà?'*[24]

Also not one to stand on ceremony without responding to Papa's greeting, Uncle Singaus said, "Avram it's time to leave Harbin. We had a few good years here, but now things are going from bad to worse. When I went to Shanghai last month... Well, I was looking into opportunities. I think my business will do much better there. The residents of the International Settlement have money to spend. There are restaurants, casinos and social clubs for people of every nationality. Tomorrow I will go to Shanghai again. I am negotiating a deal on a store on Bubbling Well Road, a major shopping street near the French Concession. It could be the perfect place for a new fur store. I will also look for a place for the family to live. The French Concession has many lovely apartments for rent. Genia and I will take Baba with us. I hope to get this all done within the next two months. As soon as we are settled, I'll find a place for you and Fanya and the children. There will be no family left here. Grisha told me last week he has made arrangements for Nehama, Tolia and himself to go to Palestine. There is a *moshav*[25] near Haifa that is eager for new residents. Hopefully, before the brutal cold of winter sets in, I will be able to send for you. Shanghai is cold and rainy in the winter, but at least you don't have to worry about freezing to death like here in Harbin."

On December 12, 1940 I was twelve years old and the farthest I had been from home in Harbin was Sun Island in the middle

---

24 Russian for 'Good evening. How are you?'.
25 Cooperative agricultural community of individual farms started by the Labour Zionists.

of the Sungari River. I sat gazing out the window of the train, alongside Mama, Papa and Teva, taking in the changing scenery as we headed south toward the port city Darien, the half-way point in our almost 1,400 mile journey to Shanghai. The landscape was dotted with poor Chinese farmers in quilted jackets, bent over, baskets on their backs, harvesting their crops, focused on survival as the train sped by. As sad as I was about leaving all that was familiar in Harbin, my heart was racing with excitement. Harbin, the 'Paris of the East', with its European style buildings, food and culture had lost its patina, and now quickly faded into the distance. Shanghai, an international city teeming with people from all over the world, would be the next big adventure. Our Betar leader, Yaacov, had shared many stories from his school days in Shanghai. Our eyes would widen into saucers as he told us about Shanghai: the lights, the trolley cars, the traffic, the rickshaws, the incredibly tall Sikh policemen, and people of every nationality. Harbin now seemed small and backward. It was a city of mostly poor Chinese, White Russians, Japanese occupiers and us, Russian Jews. In Shanghai there were the British, the French, the Dutch, the Americans, the Baghdadi Jews from the Middle East and India, the refugee Jews from Austria, Germany, and Poland, and of course the Chinese, at all levels of society. All were making the best of life, living every possibility, despite the Japanese occupation forces who had a presence in the city since 1937. In Darien we would board a steamer that would take us across the Yellow Sea and thirty miles up the Whangpoo River to the port of Shanghai.

CHAPTER EIGHT
Amazement
Shanghai December 1940

A cold hard December, rain pelted the deck of our boat, as the steamer made its way up the Whangpoo River. Hundreds of gray sampans, their ragged and sagging sails, weighed down by the unceasing downpour, lined the banks of the river. But the low-hanging clouds could not disguise the towering buildings of the Bund. Their Art Deco and Neo-Classical forms were an impressive sight, like nothing that we had seen before. We were not the only boat on the river. There were dozens of vessels of every shape and size heading west along the river, some with cargo from all over the world being moved to and from the godowns[26] on the Pudong bank of the Whangpoo. Many of the godowns had the names of British, American, French, and Dutch companies painted on their large flat windowless sides. Even more ships were heading east out towards the Pacific with every commodity the Middle Kingdom could provide; tea, rice, silk, cotton, furs, spices, fine Chinese porcelain. There were motor

---

26   Warehouses.

boats, sailing vessels and fishing boats. A Japanese cruiser, the USS Wake, and a British gunboat were moored at the wharves in front of their foreign consulates, their majestic facades keeping watch at the river's edge.

My head shifted back and forth as if I were watching a tennis match. I didn't know what to look at first. I stood clinging to Papa's arm as the boat rocked gently in the slow moving water. I had a million questions. What are those fishermen catching? What is being taken off that boat? Will this rain ever stop? How will we get all our things off the boat? Will Uncle Singaus be waiting for us? How will we find our new house? How much longer? Papa covered his eyes with his hand. I believe I was giving him a headache. "*Sssh, meine faigele!*[27] All your questions will be answered soon enough. For now, let your eyes and ears take in all they can."

The boat pulled into the wharf, and after what seemed like an eternity, the gangplanks were lowered and we were allowed to disembark. A parade of steamer trunks were being unloaded from the ship's hold. My cousin Luba, wearing a bright red coat and matching hat, was sitting high on a steamer trunk that was standing on end, where Uncle Singaus had positioned her to watch for us as we came down the ramp. She waved frantically as she called out our names. "Shalama! Teva!" I let go of Papa's hand and ran down the gangplank. As we approached, she hopped down and gave me the biggest, most welcoming hug.

"Shalama, you are going to love it here!" she exclaimed. "Wait until you see the new apartment! And the Shanghai Jewish School!" Luba was even more garrulous than I!

We put our chatter on hold as a truck pulled up with the words *Kamchatka Fur Store, 1163 Bubbling Well Road* painted in

---

27 Yiddish term of endearment-"my little bird".

English, Russian and Chinese characters on its side panels. This was Uncle Singaus' new store. Teva jumped into the front seat of the truck with me and Luba, as Mama, Papa and Uncle Singaus loaded our suitcases into the truck. When it came to our three large steamer trunks, Uncle Singaus called out in Shanghainese and two Chinese dock workers approached. He handed them a few yuan and they lifted our trunks into the truck.

A moment later we were rolling through hordes of people and vehicles. The sites of the crowded streets continued to amaze. Rickshaw after rickshaw splashing up spray as their wheels spun through the deep puddles among the cars, trucks and trolleys. We gasped each time Uncle Singaus took a quick turn or hit the brakes, narrowly missing a pedestrian or vehicle. Under his breath I heard him swearing in Russian, "*cholera*[28]", "*sabaka*"[29], and then for good measure "*mamzer*"[30], in Hebrew. But, Uncle Singaus appeared accustomed to this type of driving and, thank goodness, we did not have very far to go.

We crossed Nanking Road and headed up Avenue Joffre deeper into the French Concession. Even though the sun had begun to set we could see that we were entering a whole new world.

The truck stopped at 212 Avenue Joffre and Little Tolia was there to greet us. He ushered us up the stairs to the Singaus' large apartment where Baba and Aunt Genia had been cooking all day, anticipating our arrival. The smells of chicken soup and challah were the first to engulf us. Mama fell into Genia's warm caress and I charged like a little bull into my Baba's arms. It had been more than two months since we had been separated, the longest I had ever been away from her, and I could hardly catch my

---

28 A plague on you, specifically cholera.
29 Dog.
30 Bastard.

SHALAMA

breath. "Shalaminka, Shalaminka," she whispered over and over again. At that moment, I could've been anywhere in the world. For now, this was home.

CHAPTER NINE
Arrived
Shanghai December 1940 - January 1941

We spent the night at the Singaus' apartment. You'd have thought that we hadn't seen each other in years! There was so much to talk about. For Papa and Uncle Singaus it was all about the logistics of our move to our new apartment the next day and the possibility of Papa coming to work at the fur store. Tolia enthusiastically told Teva about how many of our friends had also moved from Harbin and were now participating in sports both at the Shanghai Jewish School and Shanghai Betar. Genia and Baba were promising Mama to show her where all the shops were and which Harbin neighbors lived close by. By the time Luba and I fell into bed together, I knew the names of every classmate, every teacher and which boys were the cutest at the Shanghai Jewish School. I also knew that instruction would now be in English. I tried to imagine what this would be like, but before I could ask what would happen if one could not understand the lessons, I was fast asleep.

The sound of dishes and silverware rattling woke me the next morning. Luba was already in the kitchen helping with breakfast and the worries about how I was going to communicate in school were brushed aside as the anticipation of moving into our new home was now in the forefront of my mind. Black bread, smoked fish, and chai never tasted better than that morning, and we were well-fortified for the move, just three blocks away.

We all could not fit into the truck, so Baba joined Uncle Singaus in the front seat, while the rest of us walked to 157 Route des Soeurs, taking in the sites of the French Concession. The street was named for the *Filles de la Charite,* or *Sisters of the Poor* in English, who maintained a garden on the road.

The French Concession was so beautiful! Trees lined every street! The houses and apartment buildings were all so different. Some were red brick, some yellow, some gray; there were large windows and doorways, some arched, some rectangular. Wooden trim and eaves adorned the single-family houses.

Baba slowly climbed the stairs to Apt 20, grasping onto the wrought iron railings to pull herself up the two flights of stairs. Baba, now age sixty-seven, was showing the effects of her years of hard work and struggle. She would be coming to live with us. Aunt Genia often went to the fur store to help Uncle Singaus and the plan was for Mama to stay home and serve tiffin, the Indian term for lunch adopted by the British, to families from the neighborhood, so it made sense for Baba to stay with us. Mama and Baba would have each other for company. Papa came up with a plan to place three or four tables into a long rectangle in the front room. Word spread quickly that hot Russian style-tiffin was available at a reasonable price and we had our first source of income. Some days Baba struggled to be on her feet. She would sit at a small table in the kitchen peeling potatoes and onions. Anything she could do was a tremendous help to Mama.

Uncle Singaus could not have found a better place for us to live! Compared to our apartment in Harbin, this apartment was huge! I shared my bedroom with Baba, but Teva had his own room. The apartment was directly above the American General Store. Since the day we moved in was Sunday, the store was closed, but I pressed my nose up to the window to see all the merchandise the store carried. It looked like you could buy everything there! There were radios and fans and fly swatters and soap. But what caught my eye were the bars of Hershey's chocolate and large jars of penny candy. I immediately started computing how much of the *gelt*[31] I received for Hannukah would be used to purchase candy from the store. But, even better than the American General Store, was the Tkachenko Bakery, which also shared the building. There was a store front, a branch of this famous Russian-style establishment, and their factory. After the smells of fish and peanut oil from the street vendors; not to mention the odor that wafted from the honey carts and trash heaps when we drove from the wharf two nights before, the aromas of fresh bread, *babkas*[32], *medovik*[33], *Napolyeon* torte and *smetannek*[34] were absolutely heavenly. I was going to have to think doubly hard as to how I was going to spend my gelt as the smells of the bakery followed us up the stairs. From our front window we could see the lovely garden maintained by the Sisters of the Poor. I couldn't wait to see what would be blooming as spring approached.

---

31 Yiddish for 'money'-Traditional gift to children on the Hanukkah holiday.
32 Sweet braided cake.
33 Honey cake.
34 Traditional Russian layer cake.

CHAPTER TEN
Impressions
Connecticut 2003

"You know Cara, I can't even begin to explain the feelings that overcame me those first few days in Shanghai. It was excitement, it was anticipation, it was a new life. Yet, it was a homecoming. We were reunited with our family. We felt safe, but there were challenges ahead. We just didn't know what they would be.

"What was the biggest change?"

"We had to learn English! For school, in stores. There was no getting around it. It was the lingua franca of the International Settlement and all business was conducted in English. Once you learned English, you could communicate with practically anyone. The Chinese spoke Pidgin English with us. The Chinese people seemed to adapt quickly to whatever came their way. They were given no choice, if they were going to feed their families. They learned what the foreigners needed and found ways to provide it. Even though we had very little money we were able to pay the Chinese to do some of our cleaning and laundry. The foreign families who were a little better established had amahs[35]

---

35   Nannies.

to take care of their young children. The wealthy had servants galore. When Papa and I were first married we had five servants! A cook, a butler, a chauffeur, a housekeeper and a gardener. Our cook, Sasha, was a magician in the kitchen. Of course, Sasha wasn't his real name. He had worked previously for a Russian family and that is what they called him. He was a vegetarian and had never tasted meat, yet we could describe any European style dish to him, and magically, it came out perfectly!

"Tell me more about your school in Shanghai," said Cara.

"It would be my pleasure!" responded Shalama.

Chapter Eleven
Shanghai Jewish School
January 1941

We celebrated the New Year in true Russian fashion. New Year's Eve started with dinner at the Singaus' apartment. The table was set for thirty to forty people with bottles of wine and vodka at each end. There were large bowls of potato and cabbage salads. Sliced meats were arranged decoratively on serving platters. *Holodetz*[36] topped with hard-boiled eggs was cut into small squares, its blocks stacked into a pyramid. Small dishes of horseradish and mustard, and of course black caviar, were next to the basket piled high with thick slices of dark brown bread. Big chunks of pickled herring were immersed in brine in one tureen, while in another, the herring was drowning in sour cream. And these were just the appetizers! Conversation, singing, and storytelling went on for hours before the main meal of latkes[37] and the brisket was finally served. Uncle Singaus had hired an accordionist whose deep baritone voice bellowed songs in Russian. Most everyone seemed to know the words to

---

36 Jellied calves feet.
37 Potato pancakes.

the songs and joyfully sang along as the troubadour circulated around the room. When he sang a love song he closed in on one of the babas or aunties, shamelessly flirtirg with them, attention that was willingly returned. When the main meal had been cleared, the chairs were pulled away from the table, the table pushed up against the wall and the dancing commenced. The men took the floor first, crossing their arms on their chests and performing the *kazatzka*,[38] squatting low to the ground while kicking their legs out in front of them. A few of the talented, more able-bodied young men balanced a bottle on their head as they carefully maintained their posture to prevent the bottle from crashing to the floor. The men danced to exhaustion and then the women formed a line and slowly, a graceful Russian folk dance took shape, their hands gesturing in unison as they moved about the room. We children were not to be denied. The accordionist burst into the music of a *hora*[39]. We formed an inner and outer circle. As the inner circle traveled clockwise, the outer circle traveled counter-clockwise. With each repetition of the verse the circles reversed direction, causing the wild yanking of the arms of the younger children by the older children in an effort to get them to travel in the correct direction. The music became faster and faster until we could no longer keep up and collapsed onto the floor, laughing and breathing heavily.

Once again, the tables and chairs were returned to the center of the room and delicious cookies and honey cakes were served with shots of schnapps.

The festivities continued on New Year's Day as we strolled the neighborhood, visiting with friends, wishing them a "*Slovim Godom*" [40]as they offered us chai and sweet cakes. Fortunately,

---

38 Traditional Russian folk dance.
39 Traditional Jewish celebratory circle dance.
40 Happy New Year in Russian.

SHALAMA

New Year's Day was on Wednesday in 1941 and we had plenty of time to rest before our first day at the Shanghai Jewish School the following Monday,

We walked along Avenue Foch from the French Concession to reach the school on Seymour Road in the International Settlement. The majestic Ohel Rachel Synagogue shared the block with the modern-looking two-story rectangular building that had been built by the Sassoon family in 1932. The Sassoon were Iraqi Jews who arrived in Shanghai in 1848. They had fled Iraq to Bombay, India and began trading with China during the Opium Wars. The Sassoon, along with other prominent families, notably the Kadoorie and the Hardoon, had continued to accumulate wealth and had built both the synagogue and the school. Their altruism did not stop there. Along with the rest of the Sephardi[41] community, they had set up a relief committee, providing dormitories, soup kitchens and medical facilities to assist those Jews who were able to flee to Shanghai from the Central European countries before being deported to concentration camps. An entire floor of the Embankment Building, an impressive Sassoon property on the Bund, was the reception center for the refugees and with the help of the Jewish Joint Distribution Committee and the brave efforts of their representative, an American woman named Laura Margolis, the refugees were registered and temporary housing was set up in Hongkew and at the Broadway Mansions Apartments. Trucks and buses were waiting at the wharf to receive the refugees as they disembarked from the *Conte-Verde, Conte-Bianco, and the Conte-Rosso,* small luxury liners, owned by the *Lloyd-Triestino Lines* that had been making the trips from Genoa and Trieste to Shanghai since 1934, bringing businessmen and tourists to the

---

41 Jews who originally hailed from the Middle East.

Far East. Each successive arrival now carried more and more refugees.

Papa, Teva and I arrived at the Shanghai Jewish School and entered the brick-clad building through the main entrance. An eight-foot wrought iron fence surrounded the campus of the school and the Ohel Rachel Synagogue with a heavy gate that swung closed behind us. A single street vendor stood to one side of the gate. His cart held a wide assortment of exotic snacks including pickled radish and roasted crickets. At recess, boys and girls from SJS thrust their hands through the fence, offering the vendor a yuan for one of his tasty treats.

A Star of David and the words Shanghai Jewish School were intricately carved above the wooden doorway. The words *Beit Midrash*[42] appeared just below in Hebrew characters. We followed the gray and red mosaic tiles up the steps into the hallway of the first floor. On either side of the hallway were built-in wooden lockers. The first room on the right was the headmaster's office. Papa rapped gently on the door and we heard a voice in English with a heavy British accent say, "Come in," we assumed, since we did not speak a word of English. Mr. Radet saw the confusion on our faces and Papa asked *"Gavareet Ruski?"* Mr. Radet seamlessly slipped into Russian. Uncle Singaus had spoken with Mr. Radet before the New Year to inform him of our arrival. Teva was now ten years old and would attend Form Three. I was almost thirteen and was placed in Form Six.

The fact that we spoke no English was going to be a problem. We also had classes in Hebrew, but all our reading, writing, math, science and geography was taught in English. We were lucky that we had studied Hebrew in Harbin, but needed to adjust to the Sephardic pronunciation of names and in prayers.

---

42 House of Study.

SHALAMA

Papa ended up hiring a private tutor for Teva and me, a Russian girl from the high school whose family had been in Shanghai since the 1920s. Her name was Natasha and she would be at the apartment two or three days a week when Teva and I arrived home from school for the rest of the semester. Baba would greet us with kisses on both cheeks and Mama would have brown bread and tea ready for us on the dining room table. Natasha would spend the next two hours giving us English lessons and helping us complete our homework. It was hard work but we persisted. By the end of the semester, just in time for summer, we no longer needed Natasha. Like most children, we quickly picked up the language of our friends.

Every part of that semester promised to be an adventure. On that first day, Mr.Radet walked us to our classrooms, leaving Teva at the Form Three classroom, and then accompanying me to the Form Six classroom. Can you imagine my shock, amazement and delight when there in my classroom was Musia Shpunt, my friend from Harbin? After leaving Harbin in 1932, when the floods destroyed her family's grocery store, they had found a storefront in the French Concession with an apartment upstairs. Shpunt Delicatessen was now a thriving Shanghai business! Musia's eyes widened and she called out "Shalama!" Simultaneously, everyone in the room looked from Musia to me and back to Musia as we ran to each other and embraced. Mrs. Petranovna, our teacher, asked Musia to introduce me to the class, which she did in perfect English. Mrs. Petranovna had prepared the desk next to Musia's for me. I could not have been happier! Not only had I been reunited with a lost friend, I had my own personal interpreter. Over the next few days, we were reprimanded repeatedly, as we jabbered away in Russian. Musia would tell Mrs. Petranovna that she was helping me with my work, which was sometimes true, but as you can imagine, often it was not. Musia was curious about what had been happening in Harbin since she left, and I, as always, had a million and one questions, now about Shanghai. We weren't fooling Mrs. Petranovna, she was fluent in Russian, as well. She was a kind, gentle middle-aged woman who clearly understood that Musia's attention was helping me adjust and would pay-off in the long run.

That afternoon when Papa appeared at the front door of the school to walk Teva and me home, a huge smile appeared on his face as he recognized my childhood friend. He gave Musia a hug and Papa said, "Musinka! How wonderful to see you again!" I could tell from his grin how pleased Papa was for me to have made a connection so quickly, and to have been reunited with a friend.

In the coming weeks Musia and I became inseparable, just as I had been with Manya. Every morning I would walk to the Shpunt Delicatessen and wait patiently for Musia to come down the stairs from her apartment. We would walk along Seymour Road, just outside the French Concession, taking in the sights, sounds and smells of the open air market.

One of our morning routes took us past the vendors who came to the market every morning at 4:00 a.m. It was a feast for the eyes! So many kinds of fish, eels and crabs! Cages full of live ducks and chickens, squawking and clucking. Some customers chose to take home their live fowl, while others asked the shopkeeper to slaughter the bird. The patron would point to the bird they wanted, and the vender would place it with its neck centered on the chopping block. Within the wink of an eye, the razor sharp cleaver came down in one fell swoop. The deceased bird would be placed on the large balance scale, the beads of the abacus would quickly fly from one side of the rod to the other and the merchant would announce the price. The customer always seemed to think the price was too high and the bargaining would commence. This could go on for some time, often erupting into raucous arguing that included accusations of cheating and swear words. The customer would threaten to leave and buy from another vendor, and immediately the price would be dropped by a few yuan. When a price was finally agreed upon the bird would be wrapped in newspaper, detached head and all, and the customer moved on to the next merchant, maybe purchasing some eggs, or any of the wide variety of fruits and vegetables available at the various stalls.

The street market would shut down around 10:00 a.m. until the next morning. The street scene on the way home had its own allure. The vendors had been replaced by food vendors pushing small carts containing charcoal stoves. On the metal top surface were pots filled with boiled noodles. For two or three yuan we would purchase a bowl and quickly slurp up the hot liquid and delicious noodles. When we finished, we returned the bowl to the vendor, he wiped it out with a rag, and returned it to his stack to await the next customer. We never gave a second thought to the fact that these bowls weren't washed between customers. Another favorite, especially during the cold, damp winter months were the roasted chestnuts that were available on almost every corner. Again, for just a couple of yuan, the vendor would fashion a cone of newspaper and fill it with the hot roasted nuts. Most days Musia and I would have to rush home, she for her piano and ballet lessons, and me for my English tutoring. But at least once a week, we would dawdle along Seymour Road and enjoy an after-school snack of noodles or chestnuts, as we discussed who we hoped to dance with at the Purim party coming up in March, or which Betar sporting events we would be attending on the weekend.

Chapter Twelve
Paradise Lost
Shanghai December 1941

That first year in Shanghai was nothing short of wonderful. Old friends, new friends, a vibrant city, holiday celebrations, so much to do. The entire school would attend special services in the magnificent sanctuary of the Ohel Rachel Synagogue before the school closed for the actual holiday observance. Our favorites were Purim in the spring and Simchat Torah in the fall. When the book of Esther was being read from the *bimah*[43] on Purim, we tried our best to compete with the boys sitting in the pews on the floor of the sanctuary in drowning out the name of the villainous Haman and his sons. We were seated in the women's gallery that surrounded the outer edge of the huge sanctuary two flights up. When we arrived at the synagogue, we girls would charge up the stairs to insure we had a seat at the railing to have an unobstructed view of the events below. In the fall for Simchat Torah, we were each handed a flag with a picture of Jerusalem and an apple, which we skewered onto the wooden

---

43   Altar.

flag stick, as we entered the synagogue. We paraded around the synagogue seven times with the adult men carrying the thirty Torahs housed in the ark at the Ohel Rachel, voices raised in joyous song, waving our flags as we celebrated the conclusion of the reading of the Torah for the year and the beginning of the readings for the New Year. On our way out the door we were each handed a small bag containing an orange, raisins and nuts, which we nibbled as we strolled home.

Every day there were choices of where to go and what to do. If we didn't have an event on any one day, you can be sure we were busy planning for the next party, holiday or outing. We meticulously picked out our most fashionable outfits and scoured magazines for the latest in hairstyles. The circle of friends continued to grow. We attended parties at the Shanghai Jewish Club. Everyone, from the Shanghailanders[44] to the refugees from Central Europe, all gathered to celebrate every holiday and on weekends to enjoy each other's company. Despite the presence of the Japanese in Shanghai since 1937, there was minimal interference in our daily lives.

Everything changed on December 8, 1941. It was 4:00 a.m. Monday morning in Shanghai when the Japanese bombed Pearl Harbor in Honolulu, Hawaii. (In Hawaii it was 8:00 a.m. Sunday, December 7.) As we got dressed for school that morning, word had already spread that the Americans were now at war with the Japanese. Japanese gunboats came up the Whangpoo River and demanded surrender from the American gunboat and the British gunboat anchored in front of their consulates. The British commander refused, the Japanese fired on the boat and sank it; six sailors lost their lives. The American commander chose to surrender and no lives were lost.

---

44   Foreigners living in Shanghai.

Despite this news and activity, we went to school that day as if it were a normal day. No one knew what to make of this latest development, so everyone made every effort to stay calm and conduct business as usual. I grabbed my coat and my school bag and ran down the two flights of stairs to go pick up Musia so we could walk to school together as we always did. From the top of the stairs I heard Mama's voice call out, *"bud ostarozehn,"* be careful, before the heavy metal door that led to the street slammed behind me.

Musia was waiting for me on the sidewalk in front of Shpunt Delicatessen.

"Shalama, did you hear the news?" Mussia blurted out the moment she saw me. "The phone has been ringing all morning."

"Of course, I did! The radio is blaring in every apartment." Our apartment complex, Brooklyn Court, was owned and managed by Asia Realty Company, an American firm, so a number of our neighbors were Americans living and doing business in Shanghai. Papa said they had a lot to worry about now that the Japanese would be taking control of the city.

As Musia and I exited the French Concession, we immediately saw Japanese soldiers with bayonets on almost every corner. For the most part they stared straight ahead and totally ignored us. We walked quickly and spoke little. We couldn't help but notice that every time a Chinese person passed a soldier they would shout out some angry sounding remark or command, often shoving the person or prodding them with their bayonets. Even after the person fell to the ground, the shouting and prodding would continue for no apparent reason. It was horrible to watch this treatment of the Chinese people.

We approached Seymour Road to see barbed wire barricades blocking the intersections. When the Japanese soldiers saw our book bags they allowed us to pass and we arrived at school without further incident. This would not always be the case. In the days to come, we might be waiting at the barricades for an hour or more, as each individual's identity card was examined before being allowed to pass. Armbands were issued to many of the residents of the International Settlement; Americans wore the letter *A*, British and Belgians wore the letter *B*, and those from the Netherlands wore an *N*.

For the first week after Pearl Harbor, classes continued without much change, but by the second week this was not the case. Our British headmaster, Mr.Radet was sent to the Lungwa Internment Camp outside of the city. Mr. Radet wasn't the only headmaster who was interned. Frank Cheney of the American School suffered the same fate. Many of the faculty of these schools were quickly repatriated to their home countries or also faced internment, so schools were shutting down throughout the International Settlement. Our class size swelled as Jewish students who had been attending these schools joined our ranks, not to mention the refugee students who continued to trickle in from Central Europe. Within a week or two, a Japanese teacher was installed and we were required to take lessons in Japanese language and history.

Mr. Suzuki was a short stern man who never made eye contact with anyone. He would walk behind us looking over our shoulders when we did our written language lessons. If we made errors in the formation of our Japanese characters, he always had a piece of chalk in his hand to draw an '*X*' on the top of our heads to indicate we were 'dummies'. He taught the history class in heavily accented English; the Japanese language classes were almost easier than the history classes. No matter how attentive we were, between his accent and our unfamiliarity with the names of people and places, we missed at least half of what he said. When class was over, he disappeared down the hall, never mingling with the other teachers, and we did not see him again until he appeared in class the next day.

We Russian Jews were fortunate that we were stateless and had been in China prior to 1937. We did not have allegiance to any government and did not pose a threat to the Japanese. This allowed us to remain in our homes. Changes that would affect the entire community were on the horizon. Still we were luckier than most. And every day I said a little prayer that the War would be over soon and our wonderful Shanghai would return to the way it was, vibrant and joyful.

Chapter Thirteen
Papa
Shanghai 1941–1942

While Teva and I were spending our days at school and Betar events, and Mama was cooking for the neighbors, what was Papa doing? Money was still an issue, we never seemed to have quite enough. I knew this from the conversations I overheard, despite Papa and Mama's efforts to disguise what they were talking about by speaking Yiddish. But we always seemed to have enough to eat. As the War dragged on and rationing was imposed, we even ate pork, even though Mama and Baba would call it "*myacca*", the generic Russian word for meat, pretending it was anything but the forbidden flesh of the pig. Baba said God would forgive us for not keeping kosher; it was not part of God's plan for children to go hungry. But where was the little bit of money that we had coming from?

When we first arrived in Shanghai, Papa would help out at the fur store. If a sewing machine needed repair, he was always there to fix it, but he said he couldn't take money from Uncle Singaus because of all the ways he had helped us. Somedays, I would come home from school and Papa would be there, reading one of the Russian language newspapers, Yevraeski Zhin[45], that circulated throughout the Jewish community. Papa had never attended school, having been taught at home by his Papa. Yet, he could read and write in both Russian and Yiddish.

I would lean over the back of the overstuffed armchair that had become 'Papa's chair', if he was in the apartment no one sat in that chair, not even the cat, and ask him what he was reading. Papa rarely initiated conversations, but this was the one circumstance when he would become animated. He always searched for an article about Palestine with which to begin.

"Shalama," he would say, "This is why we are Zionists! It says Jews from all over the world are going to Palestine. They are starting kibbutzim[46] and moshavim[47]. The desert is blooming. This is where we should be! As strong, proud Betarim, you and Teva will be there with them, building our own country. In a few years, the British will be gone and 2,000 years of Jewish exile will be over. When we celebrate Passover, there will be no more 'Next Year in Jerusalem!' We will be there, residents of the Holy Land, the Jewish homeland."

Papa's voice would become more subdued as we moved on to news of the War. Papa chose his words carefully in an attempt to shield me from the worst of the horrors. Despite his efforts, I was beginning to grasp the nature of tragedies that were unfolding daily throughout Europe and the Pacific. It was hard for my adolescent mind to comprehend the death and destruction the newspapers were reporting, and that was before we knew about the horrors of the death camps. In those days there were no televisions and computers that projected horrific images into your brain before you could even picture them. But the words

---

45   Jewish Life.
46   Collective farms.
47   Cooperative communities.

themselves were enough to create terror, sadness and relief that we were far away from the fighting; our family was safe. Was this true of the family that Papa had left behind in Nevel? Was he searching the newspaper for information about what had happened to them?

Mama's three older sisters, Sonia, Chaya and Etka, and their families were still in Gomel. Periodically, letters arrived, usually around the holidays, often accompanied by posed photographer studio portraits, with messages sending love and best wishes written in beautifully formed Cyrillic letters on the back. Mama and Baba never learned to read or write, so when the letters arrived, they would be waiting impatiently at the door when Papa came home so he could read the letters to them. The three of them would sit at one end of the long dining room table, Papa at the end of the table with Mama to his left and Baba on the right, both women leaning forward, elbows on the table, hands clasped tightly in front of them, listening intently as Papa read the letters. When Papa finished reading, Baba would hold the photograph that had accompanied the letter close to her bosom over her heart. She placed a kiss on each image in the picture before putting it in the wooden silk-lined box, where she kept all her photographs.

One day, I had just arrived home from school and was having my afternoon snack. I happened to stand near the table where Papa, Mama and Baba sat reading a letter from Gomel. I think it was early in 1941. It must have been winter since I was wearing my thick woolen forest green sweater. A small black and white photo of an elderly man and woman fell onto the table as Papa unfolded the letter. An emaciated man wearing a peasant cap sat next to an equally frail thin woman whose black scarf was wrapped tightly around her head and neck. The woman's attempt at a smile barely disguised her missing teeth. Papa looked at the photo quickly and placed it in the breast pocket of his jacket. What struck me at that moment, before Papa hid the photo from view, were the hollow, resigned stares of these two old people, stares that spoke of loss from somewhere very far away. He unfolded the letter and began reading. The photo was not added to the collection in Baba's box.

I should have stopped and listened when the letters from Gomel arrived, but I rarely did. I did not know the people in the pictures and there were so many interesting things competing for my attention during those heady, bustling days in Shanghai. In the evening, Baba would call to Teva and me to sit with her on the sofa. She would open the box, take out a picture and say, "This is Sonia, my oldest, your auntie, her husband and your cousins. You have cousins in Russia. Maybe someday you will meet them." She would repeat this for each one of her older daughters. We never did meet any of the Russian cousins, the family from Gomel. If I had listened more carefully, would I know something about Papa's family? At the time, it never occurred to me who those ancient-looking people in the photograph that Papa rushed to remove from view may have been.

As the weeks went on, Papa's reputation for fixing sewing machines spread. One day in the spring of 1941, Papa announced at the dinner table, "I have a job! The tailor shop on Chusan Road needs a tailor."

"Avram, you don't know a thing about sewing," said Mama as she placed a bowl of borsch on the table in front of him,

"Every time I fix a machine, I ask for a piece of cloth and sew a seam to insure the machine is operating properly. It appears Chaim Danielovich has been looking over my shoulder. Today he says, "Avram, you sew a beautiful straight seam. Betar is hosting Maccabi Games, sports tournaments, soon for all the Jewish Youth organizations that wish to participate. They have put in an order for new uniforms. I have a skilled pattern cutter. You can help with assembling the uniforms."

Mama took her seat at the table and began eating her soup. "If I had known, Avram, I would have left all the mending for you!" And from that day forward, she did. Papa's skills improved rapidly. Eventually, he was making jackets for Teva and skirts for me. Often there was extra wool or linen left from the orders that came into the shop and Mr. Danielovich generously allowed Papa to use the leftovers to make outfits for us free of charge. Papa was not earning a lot of money. After all, the War was still raging and few people were running out to buy custom-tailored clothes, but for the very first time, I saw Papa calm and content as he left each morning for the tailor shop.

Chapter Fourteen
Japanese Rule
Shanghai 1942–1944

Although we all wished each other *'Slovim Godom'* on New Year's Day 1942, the dark cloud of War was a constant reminder of the suffering felt around the world. Hong Kong fell to the Japanese on Christmas Day. Manila was next on the second of January. February brought the fall of Singapore; then Rangoon in March. The cold, damp Shanghai winter penetrated our bones and despite rationing of sugar, bread and rice, and shortages of gas and electricity, we were still among the lucky. So many poor Chinese were begging in the streets. We became accustomed to seeing wrapped bundles left at the curb for the trash collectors, babies that had died of cold and starvation. We had a roof over our heads and the Japanese, other than insisting we learn Japanese and throwing up barricades that made us late for school, left us alone. There were fewer extra-curricular programs at school and after school. Our Betar activities, especially sports, continued. We practiced volleyball on the grassy area between the Shanghai Jewish School and the Ohel Rachel Synagogue during recess so that we would be ready to compete against other Jewish youth organizations on the weekends. Holiday celebrations and social gatherings at the Shanghai Jewish Club also continued as usual, immune from the events going on in the world.

When the electricity went out, which happened more and more frequently as the weeks went by, Papa could be found in his chair, reading the paper by candle light. During the winter months the sun set by about 5:00 p.m. and all our windows had black-out curtains that had to be lowered as soon as darkness fell. There was little information to share to lift our spirits, not even the news from Palestine. The radio broadcasts we were able to pick up on the shortwave were coming from Russian sources, which everyone knew were laced with propaganda, but did not disguise the devastation wrought by Hitler's armies throughout Europe.

The Jews living in the Hongkew Ghetto were now trapped. For the lucky few who had found housing outside of Hongkew when they arrived, extensions to remain outside of Hongkew had expired. Some of our classmates were from these refugee groups and were living with their entire families in single rooms without plumbing or cooking facilities, in grim, gray two- and three-story buildings along narrow lanes. They prepared their meals on hibachis fueled by charcoal. For many, this was their only source of heat. Entire buildings would share outhouses, sometimes two or three floors below at street level or on the roof of the building. Some were reduced to slop buckets that were brought down to the street each morning in time to be dumped into the 'honey cart' being pulled through the lanes by a barefoot Chinese peasant. Our classmates were able to attend school but this was only after they or their parents had waited in line for hours to receive their bi-monthly pass. The erratic and irrational Japanese Sergeant Kano Ghoya, the self-declared "King of the Jews', was known for the torment he imposed on those waiting in line for hours for the pass that would allow Hongkew Ghetto residents to go to work and school. Thank goodness, the Japanese respect for education prevailed and most students received passes. Our classmates were grateful for the hours spent in school. At least they were warm and the Refugee Committee brought in hot meals each day at lunch time. There was very little socializing at the end of the day. The Japanese curfew was strictly enforced and everyone had heard the story of the students from the Mir Yeshiva who were caught outside the Hongkew gates after curfew. They received a 'light sentence' of being thrown into jail for a couple of nights. This light sentence became a death sentence for some. A few of the students contracted typhoid fever during their brief incarceration and subsequently died. Besides the danger of contracting disease in the horribly unsanitary conditions of the jail, the Japanese were known for their brutal treatment of whomever they chose to humiliate or dominate. No one wanted to find out what punishment they might inflict upon a younger group of students.

For all the horrible things that were happening around us, the very worst day for me was January 8, 1943. Baba had not been herself for several weeks already. Some days she remained in bed, saying the apartment was too cold for her to get up. One could not help but notice how she struggled to take every breath. By that first week of January, Baba appeared to be sleeping most of the day. When I arrived home from school on Thursday, Mama handed me a bowl of chicken soup to take to Baba. "Baba has hardly eaten anything all day. Please try and get her to have a little soup. She never says 'no' to you," said Mama. Her eyes were red. She did her best to disguise the worry in her voice, but Mama was never any good at this. I knew it was more than likely that she had spent the day crying at Baba's bedside. This time I had no words to help Mama be strong. I wished she was the one holding me, comforting me, telling me Baba would get better if she would only have some chicken soup, that Baba wasn't going to die.

I took the bowl of soup and entered Baba's bedroom. I placed the bowl on the nightstand and kissed Baba on the forehead.

"Baba, wake-up. Mama's delicious chicken soup is waiting for you."

"Shalaminka? You're home. Good," she said, barely in a whisper. In the dim light Baba struggled to open her eyes, a tiny frail figure among the white linens and puffy down comforters.

"Please have some soup, Baba." Baba didn't respond and appeared to be drifting off to sleep. I took her hand to my lips and held it to my face for several minutes. Despite the chill in the air her fingers were warm. I placed her hand back beneath the blankets, ate three spoonfuls of the soup, just enough so Mama would think Baba had some, and went to the kitchen. "Baba fell back to sleep," I told Mama.

No one had to tell me Baba was gone when I returned from school on Friday afternoon. We were dismissed an hour earlier on Friday so everyone would be home in time for the Sabbath. As I walked up Rue de Soeurs, I almost collided with Rabbi Askenazi as he exited the ground floor door of our building, rushing in the opposite direction, likely in urgent haste to get to the synagogue for Mincha services.[48] When I entered the apartment, Aunt Genia, Uncle Singaus, Tolia and Luba were there with Mama, Papa and Teva, clustered on the couch together, the women quietly sobbing. Like Manya, Baba had passed away on a Friday. We would observe the Sabbath and lay Baba to rest on Sunday, in the Baikal Road Cemetery, one of the four Jewish cemeteries in Shanghai.

---

48 Evening prayer service.

CHAPTER FIFTEEN
Shared
Connecticut 2003

Shalama paused in her storytelling. She turned toward the window where the setting sun now tinged the sky pink and gray. A deep sigh escaped as she turned back towards Cara. A single tear rolled down Cara's right cheek.

Shalama reached over and hugged Cara tightly around her shoulder. "Mamale, I didn't mean to make you sad!"

"There are so many things that have happened in your life that I can only imagine. But losing your Baba... it feels so real." Shalama and Cara hugged tightly for the next few moments.

"As hard as it was to lose Baba, all my memories of her are happy ones. To this day they bring me comfort." Cara knew exactly what her Amma meant. Her brain quickly listed an inventory; not only of the incredible experiences she had with Amma and Papa, even a trip to Italy, but the innumerable hours that Amma was present for her brother David and her, providing calming care and comfort. Cara always knew how much her grandparents loved her but until that moment had never thought how wonderfully safe she always felt when she was with them.

"When Papa and I went back to China in 1998, I hoped that we would be able to visit Baba's grave. We were given the name of an Israeli who gives tours of Jewish sites in Shanghai. When we contacted him, he told us a Jewish Cemetery was established in 1958 when the tombstones from the four existing Jewish cemeteries were moved to the site of what is now a Muslim cemetery. The Jewish cemetery was destroyed during the Cultural Revolution and some of the stones were used to build houses in the surrounding villages. He said he also found stones used as the lining for drainage channels, a well cover and several partially buried stones littered throughout a backyard. Such disrespect! This was not the Shanghai we knew before the communist takeover."

"What was it like after Baba passed?" asked Cara.

"There were changes. Losing loved ones during times of war does not allow much time to grieve. If you want to survive, you move on. It's strange, but you still have to worry where your next meal is coming from. As you can imagine, we prepared ourselves for the toll Baba's death would take on Mama. But she surprised us."

"How so," asked Cara?

"Yes, let's get back to the story," replied Shalama.

CHAPTER SIXTEEN
Growing Up
Shanghai 1943-1944

We prepared for Baba's funeral before sunset on Friday. Shivah began after sunset on Saturday and continued until the following Friday. Of course, the Singauses were with us most of the time. Mama and Aunt Genia sat on wooden boxes as a symbol of their grief and the pain of mourning. All the mirrors were covered with table clothes so we would not see 'the face of death'. Teva and I stayed home from school and neighbors and friends came to visit throughout the day, bringing more food than could possibly be consumed despite the wartime rationing. No doubt there were more than a few black market connections that helped to obtain the essential ingredients for all the delicious Jewish and Russian dishes we loved. I caught Teva, now almost twelve-years-old, in the kitchen more than once, helping himself to chunks of noodle kugel and babka. I didn't have the heart to reprimand him. We laughed out loud together as we joked about how pleased Baba would be to see this spread, especially since she was often the one sneaking us treats when Mama wasn't looking. Each

SHALAMA

evening, Rabbi Askenazi arrived to hold Minyan[49] so we could recite the mourner's Kaddish[50]. It was never a problem to gather the ten adult males necessary to hold prayers. Promptly at 4:30 p.m., friends and relatives streamed in from the neighborhood, crowding the living room to capacity, more than a few pressed up against the walls to recite evening prayers. I think Mama took great comfort in the support, and love, our community provided.

We all went to shul[51] on Saturday at the New Ohel Moshe Synagogue on Rue de la Tenant, one of the seven synagogues in Shanghai. The congregation of Russian Jews first established in 1907 built its permanent home in 1927 on Ward Road in the Hongkew district, where the Japanese now forced the refugees and the poor Chinese to live. Rabbi Ashkenazi greeted us and paid a beautiful tribute to Baba during the service, acknowledging what was in our hearts; that she was a completely selfless person who devoted her entire life to her family and every moment she spent on this earth made the world a better place.

Our walk home in the brisk January air was refreshing. It was just the four of us at the dinner table that night. Every time I looked up to see Baba's empty chair, I had to look away; grief overcame me and I fought back bursting into tears. After dinner, Papa moved the samovar from the sideboard to the table. The glasses in silver holders each had a teaspoon of orange marmalade in the bottom. As Papa filled the glasses with chai, Mama returned from the kitchen with thick slices of honey cake.

"Shalama" said Mama, "Please find a pencil and a piece of paper. We need to make a list."

"List?" Asked Papa.

"Yes, I will tell Shalama everything I need for tiffin for the

---

49 Prayer service requiring 10 adult males.
50 Prayer for the deceased.
51 Yiddish for synagogue.

week. Please pick up all you can tomorrow. Make sure you tell everyone you meet while you are out that I will be serving lunch again on Monday."

Papa looked at me and I saw the surprised expression on his face. Our eyes met, and he nodded as I began writing down the meats, breads, and vegetables as Mama recited the ingredients for the recipes she stored in her head.

What had changed? Since Manya's death, it seemed Mama needed support from the entire family to move forward with anything. This take-charge moment was so unusual. Was it because Baba's death was expected at seventy years of age? Did Mama now see herself in Baba's role? Except for the two months before we arrived in Shanghai, Mama had been with Baba every day of her life. We breathed a huge sigh of relief that Papa would be able to return to the tailor shop and Teva and I would be able to return to school while Mama resumed preparing tiffin in her makeshift home restaurant. The interaction with friends and neighbors would be the best thing for her.

Chapter Seventeen
Leaving School
Shanghai 1944

As the War raged on, with little indication of an end in sight, fewer people came to our home for the tiffin Mama prepared. Business at the tailor shop was no better. Papa said that sometimes it would be noon before even a single customer entered the shop. Suits and dresses that had seen many good years were being patched and altered in the hopes of seeing one more good season. It was rare to get an order for a new suit or any kind of formal wear these days. When I arrived home from school on a crisp sunny day in early April 1944, whatever brightness and upbeat feelings that accompanied the advent of spring were sucked out of the room the moment I opened the apartment door. Mama and Papa were sitting at the dining room table, each cradling a cup of tea in their hands. As I put down my book bag and slipped off my cardigan, Papa pulled the chair next to him away from the table and gestured for me to sit down.

"What's wrong, Papa? Is someone sick? Has someone died?"

"No, no, Shalama, *Gott zu dank*,"[52] replied Papa. "But Mama and I do have something to ask of you, something that we wish we didn't have to do. It is no secret that the War has taken a toll on us, as it has on everyone, and we are struggling to get by. Shanghai Jewish School still needs to charge tuition, which is only fair; their teachers need to eat, too. You just passed your sixteenth birthday, and Mama and I are so very proud of the independent young woman you have become. Teva is only thirteen. He has been helping Uncle Singaus at the fur store after school. He gives what he makes to us and we put it towards his tuition. Even with this contribution, we won't have enough money to send you both to school in the fall."

I wasn't really surprised when I heard what Papa was saying. Even with Mama's magic ability to make delicious meals out of practically nothing, it was becoming more and more evident that there wasn't much to be had, even on the black market, unless you were willing to pay exorbitant prices. Most importantly, we needed to make sure we had enough money to pay the rent to the Asia Realty Company, the owners of our Brooklyn Court apartment. With conditions deteriorating throughout the city, who knows where we would be able to find decent affordable housing if we were unable to pay the rent to stay where we were.

"I understand, Papa. I want to help."

At the end of May, Shanghai Jewish School closed for the summer. The first week in June I was enrolled in a business school where I learned typing, shorthand and other secretarial skills. By the beginning of September, I had my first real job in a medical lab where people dropped off urine and stool samples for analysis. With the constant exposure to highly contagious diseases in Shanghai, there was often a line out the door each

---

52   Yiddish for Thank God.

morning by 8:00 a.m. I was a quick and accurate typist and spent my entire day completing forms; filling in names, dates, addresses, symptoms and reasons for testing. By the end of the day there was a huge pile of duplicate copies of forms that needed to be filed. I eagerly awaited for the administrator in charge to flip the sign on the door to *'Closed'* at 5:00 p.m.

The void left by leaving school was momentary. In many ways it was liberating. I gave half my weekly paycheck to Mama and Papa, but the rest was mine to spend as I saw fit. I would stop by Musia's on my way home from work and we would pour over the latest fashion magazines together until it was time to go home for dinner. Now that I was a working girl, I needed to look the part. The skirts Papa fashioned for me were fine, but they needed silk blouses and matching purses and shoes. Every few weeks we made plans to go to Wing On Co. Department Store on Nanking Road on Saturday to update my wardrobe.

One of the most important additions to my wardrobe was a champagne shantung silk bridesmaid's dress. I can't even begin to tell how many times I wore that dress. Love definitely was in the air among friends and cousins beginning in 1944. Maybe it was all the talk of leaving Shanghai that had entered our daily conversations that made couples decide that it was time to get married, or maybe it was just what happened as we began noticing the boys we grew up with becoming men. But every wedding was beautiful, with fresh flowers, a bride in a handmade wedding gown, and a groom in a tuxedo. Those of us who were wedding party regulars made sure our dresses and suits were cleaned and ready to go when the next betrothal was announced.

It was about this time, when weddings were happening every few months, that I met my first serious boyfriend, Morris. House parties were popular so it was no surprise when Musia's friend,

Sammy Fidenglotz, invited Musia, our friend Beba and me to a party at Sammy's house one Saturday night in September. How surprised we were to find that the boys had hoodwinked us! There was no party! Sammy was interested in Beba, Sammy's friend Alex had been eyeing Musia for some time now, and Morris had been invited for me.

Morris was short, somewhat stocky, square jawed with dark brown eyes and curly brown hair. He was twenty-one years old to my sixteen and a half. He was attractive enough that I didn't mind his attention. Since there was no party, the boys suggested we go to the movies. We feigned anger at their deceit, but a movie was a fine idea. We went down to the corner of Avenue Joffre and hailed three pedicabs to the Cathay Theater. The movie that night was *Going My Way* with Bing Crosby, a lighthearted musical comedy that we all enjoyed. After the movie we went to the Peter Pan Nightclub for drinks and danced to a swing band. I think it was 1:00 a.m. when Morris left me at my door at Brooklyn Court.

Mama thought Morris was the best thing since black bread with creamed herring. She never missed an opportunity to invite him for lunch or dinner. She was always making his favorite dishes. I wasn't so sure that Morris was the right guy for me, but he was kind, indulgent and reliable. He was also a Russian Jew and had been supporting his widowed mother for several years now. He worked as the distribution manager at the Shanghai Continental Godown, receiving a decent salary.

Morris was friends with an administrator at the Shanghai Gas Company, owned by the wealthy Iraqi Kadoorie family. Morris mentioned to his friend that I was a skilled typist and I was asked to come in for an interview the very next week. I easily typed 70 WPM and started the following Monday at twice the salary I was receiving at the medical lab. If nothing else, I have Morris to thank for this job, a job I held until 1952 when we left Shanghai.

SHALAMA

When my seventeenth birthday rolled around at the end of March, Morris presented me with a ring, a gigantic pearl set atop of a square chunk of eighteen carat gold. It looked misplaced on my small delicate hands. Morris hinted that it was time to think about the future together, but I just didn't find him that interesting. I couldn't tell him that, so I told him that I felt too young to consider marriage. He told me to keep the ring, I think in hopes that I might change my mind. But by the end of the year, Morris and his mother had left for Palestine. I found the ring in my mother's jewelry box after she passed away. I think she was disappointed that I never married Morris.

It was amazing how we normalized our lives as the War dragged on and on, and soon was in our backyard. By September 1944, the Americans were bombing Japanese ammunition depots on the waterfront in hopes of bringing the War to an end. Air raid sirens going off day and night were a frequent reminder of what was happening all around the world. When the warning siren went off we would take shelter under the main staircase that led to our apartment. We were never there very long as we patiently awaited the all clear siren. The Japanese had anti-aircraft guns that they aimed at the American planes. As far as we knew their explosives never met their mark, but as soon as the all-clear sounded, Teva would be out the front door and down the street to meet up with his friends, Grigori and Yana, to comb the bushes for the shiny razor sharp shards of metal, remnants of the explosives that had fallen from the sky.

In April of 1945 the Japanese commandeered the Shanghai Jewish School for their own purposes and classes were suspended for the rest of the term. Unfortunately, the Hongkew Ghetto, where all the Central European refugees had been forced to live, was in the line of fire as the American bombers flew overhead. One day in July of 1944, the bombs intended for a Japanese munitions depot were released too early and struck the refugee camp. There were thirty-six fatalities and many more injured, including one of our classmates from the Shanghai Jewish school, a twelve-year-old boy. There was no more pretending that the War did not include us. Every time we ventured out we had a heightened awareness that our remote haven now had the potential of being dangerous; maybe not as dangerous as so many other places around the world, but dangerous, nonetheless.

CHAPTER EIGHTEEN
Shanghai
September 2, 1945

News of the Armistice with Japan on Tuesday, August 14, 1945, was received with jubilation in Shanghai. The people of Shanghai had been under Japanese rule since November 1937 when the Japanese attacked the city, just weeks before the Nanking Massacre. But the real celebration didn't begin until Sunday, September 2, 1945, when the Japanese surrendered aboard the USS Missouri. All over the International Settlement, the French Concession and the Hongkew ghetto, people poured into the streets. Teva and I worked our way through the crowded streets to the Shanghai Jewish Club. People broke out into spontaneous song and dance as liquor flowed freely as both men and women passed bottles of scotch and vodka from one to another. When we arrived at the Club many of our Betarim friends, their parents and other members of the community were already there. Anyone who played an instrument of any kind had brought it with them and there was no break in the *horas* and other Israeli folk dances as the musicians played *Hava Nagila* and *Mayim* over and over. As exhaustion set in, the musicians switched to

Klezmer and Russian folk songs that we sang with exuberance as we wrapped our arms around each other's shoulders, swaying to the rhythm of the music. The celebration lasted long into the night despite the fact the next day was Monday and we were expected at work. There were many vacant chairs in offices all over Shanghai that Monday.

The Japanese military that was stationed all over Shanghai since 1937 heard Emperor Hirohito announce the surrender to the Allied forces over the shortwave radios scattered around the city and quietly retreated to their barracks in Hongkew. It was the Chinese turn to dole out retribution for the harsh treatment they had received from the Japanese throughout the years of the occupation. If a group of Chinese encountered a Japanese soldier in the street they would knock him down, like a duckpin bowling pin, and roll him in the filth of the gutter. What was most amazing was that the Japanese soldiers accepted this humiliation without protest, as if the surrender had earned them this indignity.

With the end of the War, life in Shanghai reverted to the way it had been prior to the Japanese occupation. Shops that had shut down reopened. We walked the barricade-free streets by carefree day and late into the night, without fear. Our social lives resumed with gusto. But, we were Jewish and that meant it was time to think about where we were going next. We were stateless; we would never be granted Chinese citizenship. While conversation in our community included destinations in the United States, Canada, Australia and the United Kingdom, there was never a moment's doubt in Papa's mind; we were going to Palestine, the future State of Israel. Every time friends and relatives gathered, before the evening was done, the question of how we would get to our chosen homeland was rehashed and new information was shared. For the refugees from Central Europe, there were organizations that offered assistance such as the Hebrew

Immigrant Aid Society (HIAS) and the Jewish Joint Distribution Committee (JJDC) that arranged transport on US Navy vessels. Those were the lucky ones who went directly to the United States. Some had the long journey across the Pacific through the Panama Canal back to Europe to await papers in Displaced Persons Camps. For those of us wanting to go to Israel, there was the Jewish Agency and the United Nations Refugee Relief Committee (UNRRC), both of which had to wait for Israel to be officially declared a state in May of 1948, before they could assist with the visa process to get us out of China. So in the interim, we did what we always did. We got on with our lives, living from day to day, working and playing, and talking about the future.

While most people look forward to Fridays as the start of the weekend and the rest that the Sabbath brings, for me it had come to feel like an unlucky day. This time it was Uncle Singaus who collapsed while speaking to a customer at the counter in the Kamchatka Fur Store. Although an ambulance was called that took him immediately to the Jewish Hospital, he had suffered a massive heart attack and was dead on arrival. Papa left work at the tailor shop to bring Aunt Genia to the hospital. Tolia, now twenty-four, not only would be in charge of the store, but would be responsible for his widowed mother. But of all the Egudkin sisters, Genia was the strongest. Kamchatka Furs was closed for the week of shivah and opened bright and early the following Monday morning with Genia behind the counter welcoming customers.

Chapter Nineteen
Working Girl
Connecticut 2003

"Amma, you were only sixteen years old when you went to work full-time? Didn't that feel strange? You were so young."

"Yes, I was young, but it did not feel strange. I wasn't the only one who had to go to work to help support their family. It was a different time and while it may seem young to you, at that time it was not. Our family was struggling. Teva was only thirteen, so it was important for him to continue his education. The War was still raging and we really didn't know how long it would last. We hoped to go to Israel, but as long as the fighting continued, it was not safe to travel and it was best to stay put. Shanghai was safer than many other places in the world. It was such a tragedy when the Americans bombed Shanghai in '44. It was a case of friendly fire. The Japanese arsenal was just outside of the city. In an effort to weaken Japan from all sides, the US sent planes to destroy the arsenal. Unfortunately, the arsenal was close to the refugee area and the planes dropped the bombs too soon and hit a portion of Hongkew. It was a very sad time for the Jewish Community. Here was a group of people who escaped the Nazis, doing their best to survive in a totally foreign environment, who became the unintentional victims *of the Allies, the very forces that were trying to extinguish the forces of evil."*

"I can't imagine the constant uncertainty you lived with," said Cara.

"When you live with constant uncertainty, you cease to think about it. At that time, we just felt so lucky compared to many others. We had a roof over our heads. We managed to have enough to eat, we had our family and friends. But can I tell you about the very best thing of all?" Shalama asked with a twinkle in her eye, the look she had when she knew she was going to amuse you.

"And what would that be, Amma?" Cara responded, sensing the direction her grandmother was taking.

"When I met your Papa, of course!"

Chapter Twenty
Paul
Shanghai 1949

It was Saturday of the first weekend of September 1949. There was a swim meet at YMCA and a few of my girlfriends and I decided to go and cheer on some of the boys we knew from Betar. As we walked up to the bleachers, there were young Chinese boys renting towels for a few yuan, for protection from the spray from the pool as the swimmers raced by. I got myself a towel and took a seat next to a slender man with dark hair and glasses. He wore a light-colored short-sleeved button-down shirt, open at the collar, beige Bermuda shorts with high knit socks and sandals. At first glance, by what he was wearing, I thought he must be British, but upon hearing him speak I detected a German accent. I noticed that a girl I knew from Route de Soeurs, Sophie, was sitting on the other side of him. Sophie didn't acknowledge me and I did not acknowledge her, but every so often, when the spray rose from the pool, I felt a tug on the towel and the young man would give me a smile. As we got up to leave at the end of the meet, he said, "Thank you for sharing your towel," and we went our separate ways.

SHALAMA

The next day was Sunday and the girlfriends and I decided to take a walk over to the Race Course. The various social clubs had their athletic facilities in the infield of the Race Course, and who should I see playing tennis on the Jewish Club court? None other than Sophie with the same young man. Musia and I were leaning on the fence, drinking lemonade when the young man came walking towards us. He looked straight at me and said, "You're the girl with the towel."

I said, "Yes I am, and you are the guy with Sophie." Just then, Musia saw her boyfriend Alex with his group of friends. She said "I'll be right back."

"Please, let me introduce myself. I'm Paul."

"Nice to meet you, Paul. I'm Shirley."

"Do you play tennis?"

"No, I don't."

"Would you like to learn? I could teach you."

"It's a possibility," said Shirley, "But don't you think it might upset Sophie? I'm not interested in playing second fiddle."

"I don't think that would be the case," said Paul. At that moment, Sophie appeared having changed out of her tennis whites, into a summery flowered sundress and sandals.

"It was good to see you again, Shirley," said Paul as they walked off.

On Tuesday evening I was helping Mama with the dinner dishes when the phone rang. I immediately recognized the German accented voice.

"Hi, Shirley, It's Paul. I'd like to take you to dinner. Are you free Friday night? Have you ever been to the Peter Pan? My brother-in-law was the house photographer there. It's a fun little nightclub and the food is decent."

I remembered the Peter Pan from that first date with Morris, but all I could think to say was "Sophie?"

"I told Sophie that it was time to move on. She didn't seem too upset. I think we both knew it was time to go our separate ways. 7:00 p.m. on Friday?"

I wasn't sure why I didn't ask more questions, or keep Paul on the phone a little longer to find out more about him. Truth be told, the number of eligible young men in Shanghai was diminishing daily. At the Gas Company, I was surrounded mostly by Chinese men, older than myself. The understanding was that personal relationships at work were taboo. Although there was an open friendliness between the Chinese and foreigners, and a positive environment at work and in business, inter-racial dating was frowned upon. There were a few who fell in love, but it was at a cost. It would begin with the disapproval of the parents of the young couple on both sides, but did not end there. If they chose to marry and have children, their children were not accepted by either community. In the end it was a brave and difficult choice. In the Jewish Community, we were saying goodbye to our friends and family every week, as they left to pursue new lives in Israel, America, Australia and Canada. My own brother, just eighteen years old, left for Israel, five months earlier. I heard myself saying, "Yes, see you at 7:00 p.m. on Friday."

Maybe it was his warm brown eyes, or his long slender fingers that attracted me to Paul. More likely it was how he paid attention when I spoke, as though there was no one else in the room. Paul's questions were probing but focused. He wanted to know everything about me, and now I wanted to know everything about him. Paul was from Vienna, Austria. He came to Shanghai in 1938, at the age of eighteen by himself. Paul supported himself by tutoring other foreigners' children, mostly in mathematics, and selling advertising for an American English-language radio station, XMHA. We discovered he had sold advertising to Uncle Singaus for the Kamchatka Fur store on Bubbling Well Road. Paul's parents were still in Vienna when he left. When he received word that they were being deported to Poland, he scurried to raise funds and obtain entry visas, then required by the Japanese authorities, to bring them to Shanghai. His sister, Licci, had gone to England as a housemaid. Paul sent her a ticket and Licci left London on the day war broke out there. By the end of 1940, the family was reunited in Shanghai.

Paul had worked as a teacher for the American Private School and went to college at Aurora University until 1946. Now he was employed as a lawyer for a prominent American law firm, Allman, Kops and Lee. Paul lived in the French Concession in an apartment on Rue Vallon, only two blocks away from our apartment on Route de Soeurs. Paul was almost twenty-nine years old and I was now twenty-one. I was awestruck by how much he had accomplished in such a short time under such difficult circumstances.

Without exception now every conversation between friends and family, anyone who was a foreigner in Shanghai, began with "Where will you be going?" The communist Party had taken control in May of 1949 and every day it became more evident that the advantages of being a foreigner in Shanghai were rapidly disappearing. As our conversation over dinner continued, Paul asked me the inevitable question.

"My family is going to Israel. My father is an ardent Zionist and this has been his dream since he left Russia thirty years ago. My brother is already there. As soon as he turned eighteen he was airlifted, with forty other young people to Israel. He is serving in the Air Force of the Israeli Defense Forces. Teva is being trained as an airplane mechanic," I replied.

"We have started the paperwork to go to America," said Paul. My sister, her husband and their son left in the spring of 1947 on an American navy transport, the SS Marine Lynx. They sailed to San Francisco but immediately continued on to Boston where we have family. My father's younger brother, Richard, had some connections and made it to the States just as the War was starting. Uncle Richard sponsored Licci, Heinz, and two-year-old Jack. Now that they are settled, they will be sponsoring me and my parents."

This was just the first of many delightful evenings with Paul filled with conversation about everything under the sun. We went to dinner again the following weekend and then midweek again. Paul began calling every evening and always had suggestions for our next rendezvous. A sunset walk along the Bund, cocktails with his work associates at the American Club, a Sunday stroll through Jessfield Park in the Western District, a soiree at the French Club. Paul loved to dance and there was a dance band almost every Saturday night at the Shanghai Jewish Club. Paul would drive me home in his US Army surplus Jeep around midnight. The goodnight kisses in the Jeep were gentle and sweet.

Papa would be sitting in the living room in his favorite chair reading his newspaper most nights when I returned home from my dates with Paul.

"So, Shalama, who is your new young man?" Papa asked in Russian. When Papa spoke with me, it was always in Russian. With Mama he still sometimes spoke Yiddish, if he wanted to be secretive. He still thought Teva and I didn't understand Yiddish, but he was mistaken. It was our own little secret that we pretty much understood most everything they said.

"His name is Paul Hoffmann and he is a refugee from Vienna. He's been in Shanghai since 1938. He lives on Route Vallon in his own apartment. He's a lawyer with an American law firm."

"Paul sounds like he is well established. This is the third time this week you have seen him. Is this getting serious? You know we are leaving for Israel in just a few months. It will break Mama's heart if you choose not to go with us, and I will miss you terribly, too. I ask you to think long and hard about these choices. Do you love him?"

"I think I do, Papa." Papa rose from his chair and embraced me, tenderly holding me close to his chest, stroking my hair. Holding me at arm's length he then spoke softly, "Shalama, I know what it means to leave one's family. If you can make peace with yourself and know in your heart that you have chosen the path that seems to be right, then it is a reasonable choice. You will not know if it is the right path for many years to come."

"Papa, did you make the right choice?"

"It was the right choice for you, for Teva, and Mama. I remind myself of this every day."

Papa kissed me on the forehead and we said good night as we turned away from each other towards our respective bedrooms. The dim light of the living room did not disguise the tears that rolled down Papa's cheeks. I think he knew my decision before I did.

"So when do you think your family will be leaving for Israel?" Paul asked one day in November.

"It looks like sometime in the spring," I replied. "We have received our entrance permits and are just waiting to see what transportation arrangements the Palamt, the immigration unit of the Jewish Agency, will arrange. Mama worries every day about Teva and is pressuring Papa to make the arrangements as soon as possible."

"That can't happen. At least not this soon," said Paul.

"What do you mean it can't happen"? We have been planning this move for almost two years now."

"But that's before you met me, and I love you and I think we should get married as soon as possible."

"Will you go to Israel with me?"

"I guess that is something we will have to talk about. But first you have to say, "Yes"."

The bench in Jessfield Park was tucked away under some trees. It was late afternoon and Paul's right arm was draped over my shoulder as he held me close, protecting me from the cool November breeze. I held his left hand in both my hands and stared down at those long slender fingers. He wore a gold signet ring that he brought with him from Austria, his one ounce of gold to be sold if he ever needed the money to survive. Somehow, despite some very lean and hungry days, he never had to make the torturous decision to part with it.

"Then, yes," I replied.

Paul and I embraced and after a long, deep kiss we pulled away from each other, and I grinned sheepishly and asked, "Israel?"

"I would be lying if I told you that I have not given this topic quite a bit of thought. From the moment I saw you at the swim meet, I was enchanted. Honestly, I did not think you were Jewish, but when Sophie told me you were, I felt like I had rubbed Aladdin's lamp and all my wishes had been granted. And shouldn't every Jew be going to Israel? Haven't we learned that no matter what we Jews have to offer, wherever we end up, our Jewishness will become a liability?"

"Papa would agree with you on that point," I replied.

"For today, let's just revel in the thought that we are getting married! I know the time is short before we will have to make some very important decisions, but for now, I just want to think about, once again, how crazy lucky I am!"

The following Sunday, Paul came to dinner. Precisely at 7:00 p.m. the bell rang and when I opened the door, there he stood in a gray suit, white shirt and navy blue necktie with so much in his hands I could hardly see his face. He was holding a large bouquet of lilies for Mama, a bottle of vodka for Papa and a box of French chocolates for me. As I relieved him of the gifts, I made introductions to Papa and Mama. Papa had picked up a few words of English in the nine years that we had been in Shanghai, but Mama, having spent most of her time close to home with family and friends, still spoke no English. So Papa was able to say, "Very nice to meet you, Paul," as Paul handed him the bottle of vodka, but Mama just smiled and nodded as she accepted the flowers and went off to the kitchen to find a vase.

Knowing that Paul was Viennese, Mama had prepared schnitzel and dumplings. I had to wonder if he was being honest when he said, "as delicious as what my mother makes," or whether he just wanted to garner favor with Mama, but Mama was an excellent cook and there was no doubt he was enjoying his meal. I, on the other hand, felt as though I ate nothing. I was too busy translating each question, comment and response, either from English to Russian or Russian to English.

Over coffee and strudel, another nod from Mama to Paul's Viennese heritage, Papa asked, "Paul, what are your thoughts on Israel?"

"Mr. Froloff," replied Paul. "The establishment of the State of Israel is the most important event for the Jewish people in 2,000 years. It is a necessary consequence of the horrific events of World War II. Maybe reclaiming the Holy Land and having a Jewish State will convince the world that Jews are entitled to the same respect and opportunities as all communities should have regardless of religion, race or ethnicity. If nothing else, Jews will have a place where they will not be looking over their shoulders every minute of every day."

"Would you consider living there?"

"I wish I spoke Hebrew," replied Paul, "but I don't. I wish

I had a big strong back and was physically suited for manual labor, but as you can see, I do not. Until three years ago, I was a refugee, living hand to mouth. I am twenty-nine years old. I have been fortunate to be working for an American law firm since June of 1946 and I have been paid in US dollars. When I think of my future, and my future family, I know that I don't want to be a refugee again. I suspect that this is not the answer you were hoping for, but I hope you understand my rationale."

I was slow and deliberate as I translated Paul's response into Russian. Mama and Papa listened intently, their eyes tracking from Paul to me and then back again. Mama gave a deep sigh and rose to clear the table as I finished speaking. Papa turned to the serving table against the wall, reached for the bottle of vodka and two shot glasses and placed one in front of himself and one in front of Paul. He filled each glass and both men raised their glasses. Papa said, "*Nostrovia*" and Paul said, "*Prost*". They touched the glasses with a definitive clink and threw back the liquor in one long swallow. Mama came out from the kitchen and Paul offered her a hug, which she returned. Papa and Paul shook hands as they wished each other a good night.

I walked with Paul to the end of Route de Soeurs, our arms hooked, his hand over mine. The subject had been addressed and I was exhausted. There was a sense of relief that Papa and Mama appeared to accept his response, but it was clear that no one felt particularly happy; not Papa, not Mama, or me, not even Paul. He knew what he was asking me to sacrifice. We were getting married. We would be together. Shouldn't I be elated? Would my decision cause me to lose as much as I had gained? Papa said I would know in my heart if I made the right decision. All I knew at that moment was Israel was a dream I could not realize, not if it meant leaving Paul in Shanghai.

On Sunday January 8, 1950 there was a small engagement

party at my parents' apartment. So many of our family and friends had already departed for distant corners of the world; Teva and many of our Betar friends were in Israel, Paul's sister's family had settled in Boston, Paul's cousin Irwin and family returned to Vienna, his aunt and uncle joined their younger daughter in London. Although the apartment was crowded, we all fit around tables in the front room. There were finger sandwiches of smoked salmon with caviar on generous slices of black bread. And Mama had been baking all week, all the delicious Russian desserts that everyone craved. She was never happier than when she was complimented on her creations. Paul's mother, Lili, brought apple strudel, *kugelhopf*[53], and *schwächen knödel*,[54] Austrian delicacies that were her forte. While the two women were unable to communicate in spoken language the exchange of smiles and comments of *zer gut*[55] and *ochen khorosho*[56] left no doubt about the delicious nature of their homemade delicacies. The samovar sat steaming in the middle of the table for those who preferred tea. Unfortunately, coffee was hard to come by, even though we knew the Viennese among us would prefer coffee, but there was plenty of vodka and schnapps as toast after toast wished Paul and me a long and happy life together.

On the previous Friday morning, January 6, Paul had sent a car for me and my parents. His parents had accompanied him to work that morning and we all convened in the offices of Allman, Kops and Lee on the second floor of Hamilton House, a classic multi-story Art Deco office building just one block off the Bund where Paul worked. A beautiful Chinese wedding certificate in a red silk folio embossed with gold characters, containing a pink document decorated with phoenixes and written entirely

---

53 A bundt cake.
54 Plum dumplings.
55 Very good in German.
56 Very good in Russian.

in Chinese characters lay open on the conference room table. Judge Allman, the senior partner of the firm, called *Judge* because he served on the Shanghai Municipal Council, translated the document for us. Under Chinese civil law the couple only needed to agree to be married in front of witnesses to make the union legal. When Judge Allman finished reading, he pointed out to us and our parents where our names appeared in Chinese and we affixed our signatures. Judge signed below his name and we were officially married.

On Monday, after the engagement party, Paul had two things that he wanted to accomplish as soon as possible. He had heard that the Austrian Consulate would be shutting its doors in the coming weeks. He brought our Chinese marriage document to the Consulate and presented it to the Counsel General, asking that I be granted an Austrian passport now that I was his wife. His next stop was the Russian Consulate. My father had obtained a 'Russian Passport' for me in 1945. The only problem with this document was it wasn't a true passport; it was the equivalent of a one-way ticket to the Soviet Union. Many of those who returned to the Soviet Union ended up in the Gulags for years, some never to be heard from again. Paul never entered the Russian Consulate. It gave him great pleasure to quickly drop my passport into the mail slot and keep on walking.

Now that these tasks had been accomplished, we picked March 5, 1950, for our Jewish wedding ceremony. Both sets of parents already had documents in hand to leave Shanghai, so there was no time to lose if they were going to see us get married. Mama and Papa were able to ask the Israeli representative in Shanghai to extend their emigration visas. Paul's parents were scheduled to leave in November on a transport organized by the Joint Distribution Committee. They were among those required to return to Europe, where they would be housed in the Wildflecken Displaced Persons Camp in southern Germany while they waited for their visas. It would be eight long, miserable months before they would set eyes on the Statue of Liberty in New York Harbor.

Paul had been receiving his salary in American dollars and was eager to provide us with the most beautiful wedding possible. By the time we started planning our wedding, the communists had been in power for eight months. Shops were closing and our opportunity to approach the Chinese tailors and dressmakers, artisans who had been providing elegant hand-tailored clothing to the colonial communities, and the wealthy Chinese, was rapidly disappearing. Paul was well acquainted with the black market, which was incredibly active, and somehow, whether through our friends and neighbors or through Paul's connections, there were no holds barred. My long-sleeved dress, with a high cheongsam-style collar was made from cream colored shantung silk by a Chinese dressmaker in the French Concession. She came to our apartment to make alterations in our front room, not only on my dress but Mama's dress, and the dress for Mifa, Luba's four-year-old daughter, who would serve as our flower girl. The long flowing train must have weighed twenty pounds all by itself. Most men in Shanghai owned a tuxedo or dinner jacket, since that was the formal dress etiquette of the day, so there was much less scurrying on the part of the men to have appropriate outfits for the wedding. White lilies and orchids for the various bouquets and boutonnieres arrived from the southern provinces since it was still too cold in Shanghai in early March for those flowers to be available. Mama recruited a cadre of neighbors and friends who owned food concerns to prepare food for the cocktail reception and dinner party. Our neighbors at the Tkachenko Bakery provided the classic white-tiered wedding cake and a variety of their other specialties.

JEAN HOFFMANN LEWANDA

The loyal Chinese servants and their relatives from the Singaus household were there as servers for the reception. Sevitsky, the Russian Shanghailander, who had been the wedding photographer for years in the International Settlements and French Concession, was retained to photograph the ceremony and reception, as well as to take formal portraits at his studio between the ceremony and the reception at the Masonic Temple on Route Dufour in the French Concession. There were only two months to make all the arrangements while we continued to go to work every day, and before we knew it, our wedding day had arrived.

CHAPTER TWENTY-ONE
Wedding Day
Shanghai March 5, 1950

Winter would have its last hurrah on Sunday, March 5, 1950 in Shanghai; it was a chilly but sunny day. The ceremony was scheduled for 4:00 p.m. that afternoon. Of course, I hardly slept on Saturday night. Family was at the apartment late into the evening, eating, drinking and carousing in anticipation of Sunday's big event. By 9:00 p.m. Paul announced that he was ready to pass out and was going home to hopefully get some sleep. At midnight, Papa announced, "Shalama and everyone else here need to get some rest." There were hugs and kisses and wishes for a good night as people grabbed their coats and Mama and Papa took turns escorting the more than slightly intoxicated guests to the door.

When everyone had left, Papa and I sat side by side on the living room couch. Mama began clearing the table, carrying dishes into the kitchen.

"Shalama, life is defined by change. My wish for you is happiness and I think you have found it with Paul. Soon Mama and I will be leaving to join Teva in Israel. I do wish you would be joining us as we always planned. Dreams change. My dream will be that someday you will join us in the Promised Land. Be happy, Malinka."

"Thank you, Papa. I trust that Paul has made the right decision for us for now. But, who knows, maybe next year in Jerusalem."

Papa gave a wry grin as he hugged me tightly, then took me by the shoulders and turned me in the direction of my bedroom, once again not wanting me to see the tears that were beginning to fill his eyes.

I didn't realize it was almost 9:00 a.m when I heard Mama's firm knock on my bedroom door.

"Shalama! Shalama! Of all the morning's to be lazy!" I grabbed my bathrobe and opened the bedroom door. Of course, Mama had made a big breakfast for me, as if that was what I needed that morning! "Eat quickly," Mama implored. The hairdresser will be here at 10:00 a.m. to do your hair. Luba and Mifa are coming soon, too. We will all be getting dressed here."

I am not sure why it was so chaotic, but it was. Just a constant back and forth barrage of voices shouting, "Where are the shoes? Where is the jewelry? Is this the right purse? Lipstick, last! You don't want to get it on your dress!" I had called Paul at least four times since I had awakened that morning. I just needed to hear his voice to feel assured that this was all really happening. When the flowers hadn't arrived by 2:00 p.m., I called Paul again in an absolute panic. He assured me that he had sent his houseboy to the florist and they were on their way. At 3:00 p.m. Mama and Luba stood with me before the mirror as they helped me into my dress and secured all the tiny buttons. Mama fastened my headpiece and veil with dozens of hairpins. She stood in front of me and now it was her turn; speechless and proud, her tears began to flow.

"My beautiful little girl!"

SHALAMA

Paul's escort, his friend David, arrived at his apartment at 2:15 p.m. and he arrived at the synagogue well in advance of 4:00 p.m. to see the sanctuary decorated with blue and white flags. The crowd of well wishers were there, ready to witness the ceremony. We were getting married in the New Ohel Moshe Synagogue on Route Tenant La Tour in the French Concession. The New Ohel Moshe Synagogue was an impressive building with a large sanctuary. A radiant chandelier was handcrafted by the Miller Family to hang in the front foyer. Our guests mirrored the population of Shanghai and the International Settlement: Chinese, French, British, American, Russians, Buddhists, Christians and Jews, all celebrating our nuptials under one roof. It was truly a beautiful sight in so many ways.

The limousine that was sent for me and my entourage waited patiently at the curb as last-minute hair and make-up touch-ups were necessary. I did not make the 4:00 p.m. deadline. Paul was pacing like a caged lion on the *bima*h in front of the *chuppah*, the ceremonial marriage canopy. I learned quickly that this was his nervous behavior when being made to wait, and I would witness it again many times during our sixty years of marriage. Upon my arrival at the synagogue, I took my father's arm and slowly walked down the aisle with him. Mifa looked adorable throwing flower petals with her handsome five-year-old ring bearer, Sammy, by her side. Sammy, the son of a friend of Paul, took his job very seriously as he held the pillow with our rings at eye level in front of him. Papa stared straight ahead as I surveyed the crowd, each person holding a lighted candle, a tradition that Russian Jews had adopted from our Russian Orthodox neighbors. When we arrived in front of the chuppah Papa gently kissed me on each cheek and drew my veil over my face as I took my place next to Paul. Papa took his place next to Mama facing Paul's parents who also stood under the *chuppah* with us. The beautiful baritone voice of the chazzan filled the room as he chanted the seven wedding blessings. After I circled Paul seven times, his *tallit*[57] was draped around our shoulders as we took sips from the shared wine glass. We exchanged rings and the empty wine glass was wrapped in a cloth napkin and placed under Paul's right foot. Paul raised his foot and stomped down hard, breaking the glass, the traditional conclusion of the wedding ceremony, a reminder of the destruction of the temples in Jerusalem.[58] There were shouts of "*Mazel Tov!*" from every corner of the room. The chazzan belted out "*Siman tov u' Mazel tov*"[59] and all those who knew the words joined in singing at the top of their lungs while everyone clapped in time to the music. The joyful sound reached the street and we exited the synagogue surrounded by a bevy of smiling Chinese, eager to see what was happening and join in the celebration.

From the synagogue it was quick ride to the Sevitsky's photography studio. The bridal party were loading into the limousines waiting for us in front of the synagogue when we heard Luba call out, "Wait!" She grabbed Mifa by the hand and ran her back up the stairs into the synagogue. Clearly, 4-year-old Mifa could not ignore the call of nature.

After an hour of posing and smiling we were happy to join our 250 guests at the American Masonic Club on Route Dufour for the cocktail reception. By the time we arrived the liquor had been flowing freely and the mood of the venue was warm and welcoming. Handshakes, hugs, kisses and well wishes greeted us as the crowd parted when we entered the room. As we reached the front of the room, Judge was there to greet us with his glass held high.

---

57 Prayer shawl.
58 Jewish tradition teaches it is important to remember sad times when celebrating to acknowledge that these times should never be forgotten.
59 Happiness and Good Luck.

"A toast," he bellowed out. "To Paul and Shirley! Today we have come together to witness a true Shanghai love story. Only in Shanghai! China is in turmoil and the entire world is still trying to figure out how best to coexist after a long drawn-out war. Yet, we, the longtime multi-national residents of this international city, come together to celebrate the union of this beautiful couple. To a long and happy marriage!"

  The toast was followed by the cake cutting and our first dance to *La Vie en Rose* by Edith Piaf, Paul's favorite French chanteuse. Whether it was flowers or music or walks in the park, Paul always found a way to put romantic touches on all our encounters. I loved all his European habits that made me feel so worldly. We cruised the room for the next hour accepting congratulations and thanking our guests for attending in Russian, German, English and French. There was an abundance of gifts, some of which were handed to us directly while others were being piled in the anteroom of the hall. There were dozens of baskets of flowers, telegrams and letters of congratulation from all over the world. Pillows, fountain pens, table linens, tapestries, and generous checks also were among the gifts. Most noteworthy was the tremendous amount of intricately designed silver, everything from spoons to cake servers to vases. I was going to need an extra servant, just to keep it all polished!

  By this time it was 7:00 p.m. and we were escorted to the door by our more than 250 cocktail party well-wishers. A gentle rain had begun to dampen the streets and I scooped up the train of my gown as we hastened to the waiting limousine. For the next hour, our chauffeur toured the streets of the French Concession, as the guests of the cocktail party cleared the hall and dinner was being set up for one hundred of our closest friends and family. The sun had already set, but the shadows of the plane trees cast by the street lamps on the Art Deco homes and businesses of the

Concession added to the ambiance of the moment.

I fell into Paul's arms the moment we slid onto the wide leather backseat of the limousine. He turned my head towards him and said, "Mrs. Paul Hoffmann, I do love the sound of that," as he kissed me gently on the lips. Paul knew that my deep sigh signaled my exhaustion, and he understood as we both closed our eyes and took some time to recover from the mayhem and excitement of the day. Before we knew it we were back at the Masonic Temple, again being greeted as we were escorted to the dais for a meal of more courses than I can remember. Paul commented, "There is so much food here the servants could steal half and there still would be left overs!" With the band playing everything from the waltzes from *Tales from the Vienna Woods* by Strauss to the latest contemporary music from America made popular by Frank Sinatra and the Andrews Sisters in the background, our guests did their very best to consume as much of the sumptuous feast as possible. And we did our best to stay as long as we possibly could but by 10:00 p.m. we raised our final glass, thanking all who attended, and quickly made our way to the waiting limousine that would take us to the luxurious Park Hotel, opposite the Race Course.

The wood-paneled walls and marble floors of the lobby took my breath away. I had seen the building several times from the outside but had never entered through its heavy majestic doors with their brass handles that clearly were polished every day. Paul's law firm dealings had brought him to the hotel for luncheons and meetings and once again he chose with exquisite taste where we should spend the week of our honeymoon. There were no options to travel anywhere now that the communists had complete control of the city and its outskirts. Fortunately, the elevator was working that night as we were shown to a large room on the tenth floor with a view overlooking the Race

Course. (The elevator often did not work; it was not unusual for power to be cut off to sectors of the city for several hours.) So we did what newlyweds do for the next week, occasionally enjoying meals in the hotel dining room, although the meals served in the room were much more enjoyable, and going down to the park surrounding the Race Course for walks, saving our energy, always assuming the electricity would be out, for the ten-story climb back to our room.

Chapter Twenty-Two
Newlyweds and Communist Rule
Shanghai 1950

During the week Paul and I spent at the Park Hotel, Papa moved my clothing and other personal effects to Paul's one-bedroom apartment on Route Vallon, just two blocks from Mama and Papa's apartment on Route des Soeurs. It was a small but cozy space with a window overlooking the busy street below. The ground floor was occupied by a small market on one side of the main entrance and a flower shop on the other. We were on the second floor.

We came home on Sunday, March 12, 1950, just in time to celebrate Paul's father's 62nd birthday. Monday it was back to work as usual. At 8:30 a.m. Paul's driver and car were waiting curbside to take us both to work. Paul always told the driver to hop into the back seat while I took the front passenger seat. Paul loved navigating the streets of Shanghai despite the rickshaws, pedicabs, cars, trucks and pedestrians; I'm not sure why. It was not unusual for a mother to push her child out in front of a vehicle being driven by a foreigner, then quickly pull the child away, and then claim the child had been injured in the faux accident. The best choice for the driver was to offer the mother a few yuan and then both she and the uninjured child would magically disappear down the nearest lane. Paul would drop me off at the office of the Shanghai Gas Company on Yangtze Poo Road and continue on to the offices of Allman, Kops and Lee in the Hamilton House at the intersection of Foochow and Kiangsu Roads, opposite the Municipal Building. The firm's suite of offices was upstairs on the second floor. The driver would then return to the French Concession to be available to Paul's parents, or Mama and Papa, in case they wanted to go visiting or shopping. At 1:00 p.m. the driver would return to Paul's office, swing by my office, and Paul would drive us to Mama's for tiffin. After a very filling lunch, usually of borsch, noodles, chicken and homemade brown bread we would be back in the office by 3:00 p.m. At 7:00 p.m. our driver would be back and we would return to our little apartment for a quiet dinner or maybe dinner in one of the few restaurants or clubs that were still operating. So many establishments were forced to close under the communists due to their 'bourgeois' leaning. Our social life began to dwindle. There was a costume party in the late spring at the American Club; I was a flamenco dancer and Paul was a Cossack. There was a Bastille Day soiree at the French Club in July, but these were among the last formal gatherings with friends. More and more of the foreign community were either leaving voluntarily, or forced to leave Shanghai for their own safety. Eventually, social gatherings were confined to the homes of those who were left waiting for whatever was necessary to extricate them from China.

By August 1950, Judge Allman and Mrs. Allman found themselves in the same position as everyone else, deciding whether their time in Shanghai had expired. They were close friends of Chiang Kai-shek, the head of the Nationalist Party, and his wife, Soong Mei-ling. Mrs. Allman had attended Wellesley College in Massachusetts with Mei-ling from 1914 to 1917. Both returned to China, Mei-ling to Shanghai where she met Chiang Kai-shek in 1920 (they married in December 1927), and Mary Louise Hamilton to her parents' missionary outpost in Tsinan where she lived until she married Norwood Allman in August of 1920. Mary Louise became a diplomat's wife, at first residing in the far reaches of China, but finally settling in Shanghai. Judge hated the pomp and protocol of a diplomat's life and joined a law practice in 1924. They had a lovely home with five servants, dogs, chickens and ducks on the more affluent outskirts of town. Their connection to Chiangs, as well as Judge's many other associations from his long career in China, including taking over the anti-communist Shun Pao newspaper to protect its Chinese editor, were among the many reasons Shanghai was no longer safe for the Allmans. Clearly there was good reason for the Allmans to leave China as soon as possible to avoid Judge Allman ending up in jail, a fate that had already befallen a number of American lawyers. The two other senior partners of the firm, Paul Kops and James Lee, were already gone. Mr. Kops had returned to the States months earlier. Mr. Lee, being of an affluent Chinese family, fled to Taiwan, before he could be forced to face the public shaming the communists imposed on the exploitative bourgeoisie who were made examples of as the new communist policies took effect. Over the years, Shanghai had been an open port where people entered and exited without question. Now exit visas were only obtainable when all obligations to Chinese employees and the communist-controlled governing bodies were met. Not only was there the law firm and the Allman household to be liquidated, there were the clients who had entrusted their dissolution to Allman, Kops and Lee.

As was our routine, Paul picked me up from work one day in

late August of 1950. After a quick peck on the cheek, I slid into the seat next to him, "Judge made me a very interesting proposition today," he started. "It's becoming increasingly dangerous for Americans, especially with assets like his, and his history of association with the Nationalists and other prominent Chinese, to remain in China. A number of American lawyers have already been arrested and imprisoned in the Ward Road Gaol."

It was no secret that the conditions at the jail on Ward Road were deplorable. For all that was available in Shanghai with its modern look and contemporary feel, it was never known for its sanitation. Even a brief stay at the Ward Road Gaol could end very badly.

"Since we have Austrian passports, the threat to us is far less. He wants me to remain in Shanghai to close our office and the offices of some of our clients with outstanding obligations. Here is the deal Judge is offering us: I would continue to receive my salary in dollars, half of which would be deposited in an account in the States, a nice severance bonus of several months salary, and first class passage to the States after all affairs are settled. Also, we get to live in Judge's Fah Hwa house and retain the servants and his car until he and Mrs. Allman are able to return. What do you think?"

"Well, I don't really know what to think. We don't have travel documents yet. It sounds like it could be a good arrangement for now. Shanghai is becoming more chaotic by the day so being on the outskirts might be more pleasant. So many of our friends and relatives have left already. Our parents will be leaving soon so we have little reason, other than going to work, to be close to the center of town. We might as well be comfortable while you settle all of Judge Allman's affairs."

"If we take this offer," said Paul, "We will be financially secure when we arrive in the States. I don't want to be a refugee again, scrounging my way up from the bottom. I'm thirty years old and we want to start a family. There is risk involved in every decision. I think this is one worth taking. Frankly, this sounds like an offer too good to refuse."

I couldn't contradict Paul on this. He was thoughtful in all his decisions and his experience in life and business was so far beyond mine. If nothing else, I trusted him to do what was best for us. Paul had made so many life changing choices. The only one I had made was to marry him and go wherever he decided to go.

The next day Paul agreed to be Judge Allman's representative in Shanghai so that the Allmans would be allowed to leave China. We began making plans for our move to the outer district to the house on Fah Hwa Road.

Chapter Twenty-Three
Farewells
Shanghai September–October 1950

We knew this day would come. There are certain things in life that you believe you can prepare for. You can't. The rational mind tells you can, but no matter how well prepared you think you are, you are not. Paul said he was prepared, and although his actions supported this, his countenance revealed the ache in his heart. For the time being, I was an observer, close enough to the actors to feel their angst, but not playing their role. My turn would come six months later.

Twelve years earlier Paul had stood at the train station in Vienna on his first leg of his trip to China, only eighteen years old, with his parents, bidding them farewell, not knowing when, or if, they would be reunited. This morning, September 6, 1950, as the sun peeked through the shutters of our bedroom window in our apartment at 125 Route Vallon, I rolled over to find Paul lying on his back staring at the ceiling. The summer had been brutally hot. September was now warm and damp. The navy blue silk comforter, a wedding gift from my cousin Luba, was bunched up at the foot of the bed. The gold and silver threads of the bamboo pattern reflected the morning sunlight.

"How long have you been awake?"

"Since the sun came up," replied Paul. I have been listening to the clatter and banging of every rubbish collector and delivery man that comes through the Concession."

This was the day that Lili and Oskar, Paul's parents, would be leaving Shanghai. The Hebrew Immigrant Aid Society, HIAS, had arranged for a transport that would take them to Wildflecken, a displaced persons camp in Southern Bavaria where they would await their visas to the States. Wildflecken had been a German military base that was captured by the Americans in 1945. We could only hope that conditions would be adequate and their stay would be short.

"What a role reversal," said Paul. "The situation in Vienna in 1938 was unbelievably horrific and my parents knew that they had to find a safer place for me as soon as possible. One doesn't have to imagine the result if we hadn't made the decisions we made. Knowing this will make today somewhat easier. Shanghai does not feel as dangerous as Vienna, but it is clear now that the Chinese Communist Party has a firm foothold and that foreigners are no longer welcome. There is small comfort in knowing that for once in history, Jews must leave where they have been able to build lives and it has nothing to do with being Jewish. We are white foreigners, just like everyone else. How funny is that? At least we know my sister and family will be there to receive our parents when they arrive in the States."

Lili, now fifty-two, and Oskar sixty-three years old, and beginning to suffer from symptoms of heart disease, had a difficult journey ahead of them. The War years had clearly taken their toll and this was going to be a long and arduous trip. They would take a train from Shanghai to Tientsin, a trip of 750 miles. In Tientsin they would board a ship scheduled to stop in Japan and Hawaii, pass through the Panama Canal, cross the Atlantic to Italy and finally board a train to southern Germany. It would be November before they would be in Europe to await their entrance visas to the United States.

Paul got out of bed and told the house boy to prepare breakfast. We sat silently at our small kitchen table, quickly consuming eggs and coffee, each knowing what the other was thinking, anticipating the intense emotions that would accompany the events of the day. By 10:00 a.m. we were dressed in casual lightweight clothes foreseeing the warming of the day. We drove the car several blocks to Lili and Oskar's apartment. Being that it was mid-week the Shanghai hustle and bustle was in full swing. Paul artfully dodged the street vendors and bicycle carts with their inconceivably high piles of every kind of merchandise, from sacks of rice to bolts of cloth. The grins on the cyclists' faces belied the weight of their cargo. How they maintained their balance was truly a superhuman feat. You did not want to be a witness on the occasion one of these bicycle delivery boys took a tumble. The chaos, shouting, and blaming could block an intersection for more than an hour as the cargo was retrieved. The mountain of goods was reconstructed on the back of the bicycle so the delivery boy could continue on his way. We left the car at the curb by the front door.

"*Gutte morgan*[60], *Mutter. Gutte morgan, Vater,*" Paul called out in a voice I knew was artificially cheery in his attempt to make this morning easier for all concerned. He leaned over his mother's shoulder and pressed a kiss firmly on her cheek as she sipped her tea at the breakfast table. Four suitcases stood packed and ready near the door. All their other belongings would be packed into crates and stored at a godown, eventually to be joined by our household goods waiting to be shipped to the States. I gave a brief hug to my mother-in-law and father-in-law and stepped back as Paul took charge. Oskar spoke little English,

---

60 Good Morning in German.

and Lili still did not speak English at all, so beyond a few social interchanges our conversations were limited. This morning, all communication was in German. It was obvious that there was little time for social graces and all energy had to be conserved for the events of the day.

We left the house by noon and arrived at the train station at 1:00 p.m. Considering the size of the crowd, identity checks and custom control operated with amazing efficiency. We stood in line with Lili and Oskar as Chinese guards reviewed their paperwork and their luggage was open for inspection. The regulations imposed by the communist authorities were strict as to what foreigners were allowed to take with them when leaving the country. Paul had warned his parents not to take any risks by concealing anything in their suitcases. If there were things that they needed beyond what they were allowed to take, he would arrange to have it sent to them when they arrived in Germany. The guard rifled through the suitcases containing clothing, personal care items and a few books, looking for gold, silver, jewelry, and cash that may have been stealthy stashed within. Having found nothing, obviously disappointed and disgruntled, the guard pushed the suitcases in their open disorganized state to the end of a long table. I heard Lili mutter "schweiner hunt"[61] under her breath as she struggled to replace all she had so carefully folded and packed the night before. Paul slipped a young Chinese man, who clearly was looking to earn some spare change, a few yuan and indicated to him that he should help carry the luggage up the platform and onto the train. After several tight hugs and many kisses among the four of us, our last and only words to each other were, both in English and in German, and repeated several times, were "See you in America."

---

61   German for *pig dog*,

SHALAMA

By 2:00 p.m. Lili and Oskar had boarded the train. The train for Tientsin was not scheduled to leave until 7:15 p.m. that evening, but this was a mass transport and there were so many people to process. Arriving early, before the guards were hot, tired and irritable, made the process a little less stressful and guaranteed seats. Thankfully, the summer heat and humidity had broken and Lili and Oskar would not be stuck in a stifling train car for the next five hours. We were not allowed onto the platform but were told if we came back at 7:00 p.m. we could go up on the platform to wave a final goodbye. We drove home, had a light lunch and after unsuccessfully trying to read, lay down for a nap. At 6:15 p.m. we were back in the car to the train station. We had to park several blocks away as it was clear that we were not the only ones trying to ascend the platform before the 7:15 p.m. departure. When we got to the foot of the stairs, several armed guards blocked the way bearing their rifles across their chests. Apparently, there had been an unexplained change, not unusual these days under the new communist government, and no one was allowed on the platform. Paul and I found a spot where we could watch as the train pulled away. His arm was over my shoulder, holding me tightly as the train cars left the station. Every window was crowded with faces looking out, searching for loved ones, catching a final glimpse of Shanghai. We did not see Lili and Oskar in those last moments. As the train disappeared into the distance, Paul pulled me closer, saying nothing, simultaneously conveying and containing his emotions. At that moment I realized that within a few short months, my parents would be leaving for Israel. There would be no family left in Shanghai.

"Let's go," Paul said.

"My father said he will help us empty your parents' apartment. I told him you want your Mother's plants to come to us. Papa will deliver them tomorrow afternoon."

"Tomorrow is another day," said Paul as we descended the steps of the platform to return to the car.

Early on the morning of October 11, 1950 there was a feeling of deja vu in the events of four weeks earlier. This morning we would be accompanying the Allmans to the pier in their car as they boarded *an* American military transport for the States. There was nowhere near the scrutiny and crowding that Lili and Oskar encountered when they departed just one month earlier. After all, not only had Judge Allman been in the diplomatic service when he first arrived in China in 1916, by 1925 he was a prominent lawyer. He also served on the Shanghai Municipal Council, administering international law, and with the Shanghai Volunteers, protecting the International Settlement during times of conflict. He was an avid polo player and a founder of the Shanghai American Club. As if all this was not sufficient to garner him special treatment, in the last several years he began doing work for the OSS, Office of Special Services, the predecessor to the CIA, United States Central Intelligence Service. He had become a vital link to the United States government, providing intelligence on the volatile political situation in China. After our sincere wishes for a bon voyage, and final instructions to Paul from Judge Allman, we returned to the house at 179 Fah Hwa Road. I was a little giddy, now being the mistress of such a large and fine house. Sasha, the cook, had prepared a European style dinner of goulash and spaetzle[62] for us, which Paul had requested, and uncorked a bottle of fine French red wine from Judge's still extensive store of wine and hard liquor. We sat at opposite ends of the large dining table intended to seat at least twelve as we surveyed the room.

---

62   Austrian-style noodles.

SHALAMA

I raised my glass first. "Happy 30th birthday, Darling! May we celebrate the next ninety years together, in health, happiness and prosperity with family and friends!" (A common Jewish birthday wish was, "Like Moses, may you live to be 120!", so a wish of ninety more years was not unusual.) On the weekend, we would celebrate with dinner at my parents' apartment, go to the movies to see *Cleopatra,* at the Nanking Theater and then do some boozing at a local nightclub with friends.

Paul raised his glass. "To us and to our future. This is life the way it is meant to be!" I had to laugh. I knew how much Paul enjoyed the finer things that an affluent life provided.

I raised my glass again. "To us, our future, reunited with our family and friends. And to a dining room table where I won't need to shout to have a conversation with you!"

CHAPTER TWENTY-FOUR
Crisis
Shanghai November 1950

Not long after moving into the Allman's Fah Hwa house, Paul developed a pain in his right groin. The doctors diagnosed a chronic inflammation of the appendix and recommended that he have an operation to remove it. From the very first moment I met Paul there had been life changing decisions without much time for reflection. To go to Israel or the States. To marry as soon as possible to obtain an Austrian passport. To be Judge's proxy. And those were the big decisions. There were so many smaller day-to-day decisions. Which streets were safe to navigate? Which former associate could we confide in? The decision about Paul's surgery could be a life or death decision.

"We don't know how soon we will be leaving for Hong Kong or when we will be on a boat for Europe. A ruptured appendix can be deadly," Paul told me. It is a fairly simple routine operation and there are skilled doctors here in Shanghai. I think I should do it." His reasoning was sound, so I agreed.

The surgery went well, but on the third day of recovery, when I arrived at the hospital, it was clear that something had gone terribly wrong. The doctor met me at the door to Paul's room.

"There's been a complication," the doctor said. Paul has developed a blood clot and it has traveled to his lung. The hospital has run out of anticoagulant drugs. If we don't administer some soon, his chances of survival are slim."

"What is the name of the drug?" I asked.

"Heparin," the doctor replied.

I ran down the stairs and out to the street. I instructed our chauffeur to take me to the offices of Allman, Kops and Lee at Hamilton House. Rather than wait for the elevator I ran up the flight of stairs, thrust open the door to suite 208, practically colliding with the office boy, Peter Chang, Paul's steadfast assistant. Peter read the look on my face immediately.

"It's Paul, There's been a complication from the surgery and he needs medication and they have run out of it at the hospital. How much money can you give me from the safe?" I knew that Paul had shared the combination to the safe with Peter, the only employee of the firm who still could be trusted. Peter returned with a briefcase filled with yuan bills. The value of the yuan had dropped so dramatically, that massive amounts were necessary, even for the smallest of purchases. I ran down the stairs and instructed the driver to take me to the pharmacy on Bubbling Well Road, near my uncle's fur store where the proprietor would recognize me.

I ran into the store and without making introductions, I called out to the pharmacist, "Do you have Heparin?"

"I have two doses."

"I'll take it," I said. "Where can I get more?"

The pharmacist provided the addresses of several other shops and black market dealers. After five pharmacies and two black market dealers, I returned to the hospital and presented all the medication I had collected to the medical staff. I sat in the chair next to Paul's bed, holding his hand as they began to administer the intravenous drug.

"You are not allowed to die," I whispered. "Do you hear me? You are not going to leave me in this crazy city on my own!" I felt hot tears run down my cheeks as I stared at Paul's gaunt gray face covered by an oxygen mask. Eventually, I sat back in the chair and slept.

It was sometime in the early morning hours that I was awakened by a loud raspy coughing coming from Paul's bed. I turned to look at Paul. He was half sitting up and his face was bright red as the cough became deeper and more frequent. A nurse came running to his bedside with a basin and after a few minutes, Paul coughed up a blood clot the size of a small fist. His first words were, "I nearly died now."

"But you didn't," I said. "You heard me, and you didn't." I hugged him so tightly he grimaced in pain.

The drama wasn't quite over with Paul's positive response to the medication. Later that afternoon as I sat at Paul's bedside, content to watch him breathe normally as he slept, one of the nurse's told me someone was asking to see me in the lobby of the hospital. I was greeted by a Chinese man who I recognized as a clerk from Allman, Kops and Lee.

"Mrs.Hoffmann," he said, "the employees of Allman, Kops and Lee want you to send a telegram to Judge Allman in America."

"Whatever for?" I asked.

"We want Judge Allman to appoint a new proxy in the event that Mr. Hoffmann should die."

I stared at him in disbelief. "First of all Mr. Hoffmann is not dying. Second of all you neither have the authority, nor the right to ask this of me. And how disrespectful to come at this difficult time with such a request! You bring dishonor on yourself and your family. You should be ashamed!" I turned and walked away, knowing that I most probably hit a nerve with the young Chinese man with my comment about bringing dishonor on his family. For a moment, I remembered my feeling of pride when I slugged the schoolyard bully while defending my younger brother so many years earlier in Harbin. I kept the events of that afternoon from Paul, what the employee requested and how I handled it, until he was well on the road to recovery. When I finally told Paul several weeks later, I was rewarded by the look of astonishment and appreciation on his face that was only surpassed by the knowledge that I had saved his life.

CHAPTER TWENTY-FIVE
Heroine
Connecticut 2003

"Amma! How terribly frightening!" exclaimed Cara. "Did you think Papa was going to die?"

"One does not stop and think about such things in situations like this, mamela. One never believes that their loved one will die. The realization only hits when your loved one is gone and sometimes not for a long time after that. There's that feeling that at the end of the day they will just walk in the door, just like always. Anyway, I had no one to turn to, so I did what had to be done."

"Weren't you afraid that someone would stop you, or you could be arrested for interacting with the black market dealers?"

"Shanghai still had a bit of its wild west atmosphere. Anything, or for that matter anyone, could still be bought or sold in most situations, for the right price. That is why the communists achieved their success and came to power. The chasm between those who had and those who had not was way too wide to cross. They were trying to right a wrong, but to this day so much has gone wrong for the Chinese people. The foreigners and the affluent Chinese could have whatever they wanted because they could pay for it. The system was incredibly corrupt.

SHALAMA

Meanwhile the goodhearted Chinese people were struggling just to feed their families."

"Did it make you uncomfortable to see how the Chinese lived?" asked Cara.

"Of course it did. It was not unusual to see Chinese babies that had died overnight wrapped in rags in the street to be picked up in the morning by the trash collector. We were not rich by any means, but every foreigner could afford to pay the poor Chinese for their services. We knew we were helping them survive as well. But when your grandfather became ill, I was clearly a foreigner who was going to work the system as best I could. I ended up collecting far more Heparin than Papa needed. We donated whatever was left to the hospital, which was greatly appreciated."

"As frightening as this episode with your grandfather was, it was only the beginning. We had only been married seven months, and as the communists continued their takeover of Shanghai, we couldn't even have imagined what would happen next."

"Were your lives in danger?" asked Cara.

"We tried not to let our minds go there. But there was more than one time when I feared for Papa's life."

CHAPTER TWENTY-SIX
Purge
Shanghai December 1950 - January 1951

In December of 1950, the United States Government froze all funds related to assets in China. Paul immediately sent a letter authorizing the bank in Boston to remove his name from the account where Judge Allman had been sending his salary. From that date forward all his salary would still be deposited directly into the bank in Boston and we would have to survive on my salary, which fortunately I was still receiving on a regular basis. Paul had given his father access to the Boston account when it was first set up as part of his agreement with Judge Allman. Lili and Oskar were still in DP camp in Germany, but the hope was they would be in the States soon. Paul wanted to ensure that the account would not be connected to him back in Shanghai so his parents would have access to the funds as they began their new life in America.

The situation in China was deteriorating rapidly. We were confined to our house more and more. Two to three times each week the employees of Allman, Kops and Lee, or representatives of other American firms that Paul had been tapped to shut down, crowded into his office; groups as large as twenty individuals in a space that could not hold more than eight. They would demand their 'just' payout. After several hours of demands, and Paul explaining the situation, they would insist on another cable being sent to Judge Allman in the States, a demand that had become expensive, especially repeated several times each week. Then there were the days that Paul was called to the Labour Bureau, a row of unheated shacks, with long tables and hard benches with no backs that Paul described as "frigid as an iceberg in the Arctic in winter and hot like the dungeons under the lead roofs of Venice in summer". Paul and the office boy, Peter, sat for hours, explaining again and again that when the funds were available, all workers would be paid as stipulated in agreements signed by management prior to their departure from Shanghai. When these explanations were rejected the interrogator would refer the case to the court. Repeated court visits were then added to Paul's weekly routine. These cases, as well as others involving taxes, commerce and liquidations had become his daily fare.

I saw the stress and fatigue build each day. Paul was sleeping poorly and his appetite was gone. His weight was down to 120 pounds. I did my very best to have his favorite foods prepared each day. This was becoming more difficult as much of our usual fare was quickly becoming black market commodities, if available at all. I coaxed him through every meal encouraging him to eat more of the less than appetizing fare that had curtailed his appetite. Despite the letters from Judge Allman that confirmed he was pulling out all the stops, writing letters to congressmen and the Secretary of the United States Treasury to obtain a license to release the funds to extract us from this predicament, on many days it took more energy than we had to deal with these tasks. As we collapsed into bed at the end of the day, exhaustion took hold. Ultimately our method of coping was to just go to sleep.

There was nothing left to say or do, and we had to believe that tomorrow would bring answers and resolution.

While our personal woes loomed large, the communist had embarked on a program of public displays of humiliation, which Mao Zedong deemed necessary to purge Chinese society of counterrevolutionaries. Loudspeakers blasted in the streets, denouncing store owners of bourgeois acts and crimes. Saturday became 'parade' day. Streets were blocked for miles as the masses piled onto the thoroughfares following individuals with hands tied behind their backs and peaked 'dunce caps' on their heads. A truck with a propaganda loudspeaker led the way to the local stadium where these people would be brought to their knees with heads bowed, as insults were shouted and and they were beaten. Some of these 'trials' ended in execution. Others resulted in individuals being carted away for years of re-education in deplorable conditions in forced labor camps. Rather than face this fate, suicides became common. In one month there were approximately 1,000 suicides in Shanghai alone. Sometimes entire families chose to end their lives rather than 'confess' to having knowledge of acts their loved ones were accused of, and in many cases had not committed, but everyone had to be guilty of something. We heard the blare of ambulances all day long. Even if we wanted to venture out, to our offices or on errands as we often did on Saturdays, we were going to have to make other plans.

Paul was not one to readily bow to the perils created by authoritarian rule. He had told me of more than one episode of going out into the street after the Nazi takeover of Vienna; he had quickly learned the foolhardiness of his decisions.

Paul returned to the apartment after attempting to retrieve some shirts from the laundry early one Saturday morning. He was pale and breathless. I was sitting in the living room knitting, a hobby I had taken up since both work and socializing had been curtailed and we were mostly confined to the house. I had created a list: socks for Paul and his father, scarves for Mama and Lili, a sweater for Jacky. Paul sat down next to me and after he caught his breath, told me what he had witnessed. The owner of a neighborhood provisions store had just taken his life by jumping from the roof of the building. His bloodied body lay on the sidewalk in front of the store. A loudspeaker truck had been parked in front of the store earlier, for hours blaring "Boss come out and confess. We know you dealt in foreign currency. We know you evaded taxes. We know you are a reactionary. Come out and confess!"

Moments later I found Paul at the typewriter, nervous with sweat beaded on his forehead, pounding away at the keys, composing a letter to his sister, Licci. Not only was he confirming that he had sent the authorization to remove his name from the Boston bank account, he wrote, "I have made a terrible mistake. I am a fool! What fantasy was I living to believe that the Chinese would be more Chinese than communist and Shanghai would be Shanghai again? Whatever we had here is gone. We can only hope that when we leave, we leave with the clothes on our backs and our lives."

As I read over Paul's shoulder, I said, "You can't send this. Can you imagine the fear and worry this will generate? Your family has enough on their plates adjusting to their lives in the States. What good will it do to add to their anxiety? We didn't make a mistake. When Judge and Mrs. Allman left, it was with the intention of returning and starting anew when the political situation quieted down. Who could predict it would take such a violent turn? We are just going to have to find a way to finish up here and be gone. If I didn't believe it was the right decision, I would not be standing here next to you. Just look at all the challenges you have faced so far and what you have accomplished in the last thirteen years. Your family survived the War. Your sister and family are safe in America. Your parents will be there soon. You completed your education, became a lawyer and established yourself in Shanghai. Monumental tasks under any circumstances. You're thirty years old and we have our entire lives ahead of us. This is not where it ends!"

I pulled a chair up next to Paul to help rewrite the letter. He tore the onion skin paper off the typewriter roller and began again. He left in the part about the adjustment to the American bank account, but then continued on to say that we are young and strong and will weather the obstacles in front of us, just like we have weathered so many others. He even included the hope that we might get our exit visas by March, our first anniversary, which would be a miracle. I returned to my knitting. After an hour or so, I stood up from the too soft armchair that I had been sitting in to stretch my back. When Paul had completed the letter he had leaned over my shoulder to give me a peck on the cheek on his way into the bedroom to attempt a nap. I glanced over to the typewriter table and saw the completed letter, ready to be folded and awaiting postage. I quickly read through it once again. Paul had included a final paragraph.

"There has only been one good thing I accomplished in 1950 and that was to marry Shirley. She has a character that is hard to find, and now that everything is so difficult, she is funny, content, and a really big support, as you would barely expect of someone so young and lighthearted.

10,000 kisses,

Your Paul"

Chapter Twenty-Seven
Another Farewell
Shanghai February 1951

Mama and Papa were hoping to leave for Israel by mid-January. They were all set to depart when we announced our engagement, so they requested an extension. Fortunately the Israeli representative in Shanghai was willing to extend their emigration documents. Now it was the problem of arranging transportation. The Joint and Palamt were doing their best organizing flights out of Shanghai, but were limited to one transport flight per month. At first Mama and Papa were informed that they would depart on January 18, 1951, but two days later they received word that the flight was full and they were waitlisted for the next flight, which would be some time in February. I saw the disappointment on Papa's face. He was eager to reunite with Teva. It was approaching two years since Teva had left to serve in the Israeli Defense Forces. Papa was so very proud that Teva had inherited his mechanical skills and was training as an engine mechanic in the Air Force. Tears flowed freely from all of us the day Teva left, especially from Mama, of course. He was eighteen years old and had never lived anywhere else except with Mama and Papa. I thought Mama was never going to release Teva from her hug as he lined up to join the group of forty young men boarding the cargo plane bound for Tel Aviv. Finally, by the end of January, Papa and Mama received word. It was confirmed that they would depart Shanghai the morning of February 15, 1951.

A flurry of new activity began, once again. Mama's moods were completely unpredictable. Some days when I arrived to help with the packing, she was busily involved in folding linens and clothing, placing them in the two exquisitely carved wooden chests Papa had purchased in Shanghai during the War years that would be shipped by boat, hopefully arriving in Haifa not too long after they did. While Mama and Papa would be traveling by plane, upon arrival in the port of Haifa their household goods would be trucked to Moshav Beit She'arim, north of the city. Relatives, the Davidoviches, cousins on Fanya's side of the family, had settled there and had secured housing for them. On the good days Mama was eager to discuss what the future would be like on the moshav, reunited with family. On those days she was upbeat and positive. If nothing else there was her eagerness to see Teva, who was very much still her little boy, and this outweighed whatever fears she was harboring about this next major transition in her life. Fanya could hardly remember the train ride across Russia from Novozibkov to Harbin when she was a little girl. The move to Shanghai in 1940 seemed huge at the time, but small to what was in front of them now. The thought of never having to experience cold weather again sounded wonderful, and although Genia and family were on their way to California, Nehama, Grisha and Tolia were in Israel. And Israel was Avram's dream. She would not deny him this.

On other days, I found her sitting in a darkened living room, weepy and red eyed. Often this was on a day when a letter had arrived from Teva describing the difficulties of living in the nascent State of Israel. His letters were filled with the challenges of food shortages, power outages and Arab insurrections. No one expected creating a Jewish state in the middle of a hostile desert was going to be easy. Despite the will power and resilience of our people, reports of daily events in Israel often came as a shock. After all these years of turmoil and threat in China, with the imminent loss of all we owned since the takeover of China by the communists, you would think Mama would let the positives outweigh the negatives, see the bright side of their impending move, but this was not how Mama rolled.

Had Mama ever lived in peace and prosperity? Truth be told, only for a few fleeting months at a time. Whenever it appeared as though our family situation was on an upswing; when we first moved to Shanghai and then during Shanghai's rebirth immediately after the War; within a blink of an eye her fragile universe was disrupted again. Events that were so beyond just us, events that would change the course of history, inevitably changed our lives too. Having our tiny tastes of life as it should be, we had made the most of what we had. We were constantly reminded of how incredibly lucky we were to be surrounded by family and friends while others had suffered such devastating losses. I did my best to remind Mama of this and hoped the next day when I arrived an optimistic, cheerful Mama would meet me at the door. I took some comfort in knowing that they were leaving before us and going to where there was the support of family, even if conditions were less than ideal. I couldn't even begin to imagine the scenario if we were to leave first. Poor Papa, strong as he was, would have been trying to keep Mama on an even keel within the shrinking bubble the communists had created for foreigners. I would miss them, but I was so relieved that they were liberated from what life in Shanghai had become.

JEAN HOFFMANN LEWANDA

We were young, strong, and savvy and much better suited to face the uncertainty of the coming months. As Paul and I stood on the tarmac, watching as the plane faded into the distance, my deep sigh sounded like a sigh of relief, but it was not. It was recognition that our family was moving on, and acceptance of a profound sense of loneliness. All of our family had departed, leaving us on our own in Shanghai, with a single goal, finding a way out of China.

Chapter Twenty-Eight
It's Over
Shanghai February–March 1951

It was a warm day at the end of February. The skies of Shanghai were overcast as the setting sun did its best to shed a glimmer of light between the downtown skyscrapers. Paul had called me earlier in the afternoon to inform me that he was going to be late picking me up from work that evening. I sat at my desk flipping through a dog-eared copy of Life Magazine from November 1949 with a very dapper Ricardo Montalban, 'Hollywood's New Romance Star', on the cover. It had been passed around the office to so many of our staff, it was beginning to fall apart. It was well past 7 p.m. and I knew this was not a good sign. If nothing else, Paul was always prompt, and usually hungry for dinner. His being this late did not bode well for whatever news he would have to share this evening. At 7:30 p.m. I heard the sound of the car horn. The magazine fell open on my desk, I grabbed my purse and jacket, and ran out to the car. As usual, the chauffeur was in the backseat and I slipped into the passenger seat next to Paul.

Paul was never one to disguise his emotions and I could tell immediately from the tension in his face that it had been a difficult day.

"What's wrong?" I asked.

"Is it that obvious?" Paul retorted more curtly than I expected.

"The sojourn in Judge's residence is officially over. I was informed today by the communist Party observer that on Monday the local Party officials will appropriate Judge Allman's house and anything else he and Mrs. Allman left behind. We have the weekend to see what we can save. That doesn't give us much time. The servants know what is in the house and if they have shared this information with any of the Party officials, or for that matter any of the neighbors, I could end up in jail for concealing assets."

From the moment Judge had appointed Paul to be his proxy, a communist Party observer had been assigned to him. The small stern-faced man of about fifty years of age donned a worn gray western suit. He was at the office when Paul arrived in the morning and left the office as the lights were turned off each evening. He reviewed every letter or document that touched Paul's desk. He listened in on phone calls and personal conversations. If Paul had to visit a client, or was called to a court hearing, there was the observer following two steps behind Paul and Peter Chang, the trustworthy office boy and translator. It was unclear how much English the observer understood. If he had a question, he would address Peter in Chinese, and Peter in turn would direct the question to Paul in English. Whether Peter translated exactly what Paul had said, we never knew. What we do know was that Peter was excellent at mitigating and mollifying. Once the observer heard what Peter had to say, he usually seemed satisfied and they moved onto whatever was next.

It was late November of 1950 when China entered the war in Korea. It was no surprise to those of us living in Shanghai.

We saw the Chinese troops marching through the streets. If you asked them where they were going, they would say Korea. Yet the Americans acted surprised. General Douglas McArthur later testified in front of Congress that his troops were caught off guard by the arrival of the Chinese in Korea. It seems incredible that McArthur did not know what was common knowledge to the average citizen on the streets of Shanghai; and these events would have a tremendous impact on our lives.

The United States Treasury had continued the freeze on all funds intended for China for three months now. Monies that were supposed to pay employees of Allman, Kops and Lee, US Shipping Lines, a number of other clients, and settle the Allman household were still inaccessible. Paul was responsible for the salaries of seventy people and there was no money to pay them.

The first thing to go was the car, which was relatively easy to sell quickly, Then there was Judge's considerable stash of liquor. A black market trader showed up on Sunday and quickly hauled most of it away. The servants made themselves scarce while this was going on. They must have figured out if the authorities knew about the liquor, they would confiscate it. If the liquor was sold, the servants had a better chance of being paid. Thank goodness they remained quiet and pretended to ignore the boxes being carted out the back door of the house. On Monday morning, Paul lined the servants up in the front foyer of the house, handed them envelopes, thanked them for their service and sent them on their way. By Tuesday morning, we had packed our personal belongings. At noon, an official of the communist Party was on the doorstep reading a proclamation that the house at 179 Fah Wah, which had belonged to the American 'capitalist running dog' Norwood Allman, was now the property of the Chinese people. My cousin, Tolia, had arranged for a truck from the fur store to pick us up, and what personal belongings were left, and deliver us to a two bedroom apartment nearer to the center of town. We would be sharing the apartment, a far cry from the house at 179 Fah Wah, with our friends, David and Bella Vilenzky and their school age son, for the next twelve months.

Chapter Twenty-Nine
Prisoners
Shanghai Spring 1951

While I went to work every day at the Shanghai Gas Company, Paul usually could be found at the office or in court with Peter by his side. Frequently, Paul was called to the police station or the Labour Bureau to address some matter and Peter would accompany him there as well. It would have been foolhardy to attempt any negotiations or proceedings without a fluent Chinese speaker. Why Peter did not waver in his loyalty, we never knew. He was the only employee at Allman, Kops and Lee that did not harass Paul about not being paid. For all we know, he may have saved Paul from imprisonment when he chose his words wisely in the interactions with the observer, the police, the inquisitors at the Foreign Affairs Bureau, and judges when Paul was summoned to appear in court. Paul's letters to Judge Allman were no longer restrained. He wrote to Judge Allman of "relentless persecution by disgruntled employees" and the fear that the employees would "kill me or drive me crazy." It seemed like every few days we received a copy of a letter that Judge had written to the federal officials in the States and the officers of the US Lines, imploring them to intervene on our behalf.

On April 15, once again I found Paul at the typewriter. There still was no license and no funds to pay off the employees of

US Lines or Allman, Kops and Lee. The US Lines employees were accusing Paul of using funds intended for them to pay off law office employees. The Chinese refused to issue us exit visas because the obligations had not been met. Time to receive American visas as Displaced Persons was running out. If we did not pick up our visas to enter the States by June 30,1951 in Singapore, we would have to enter the quota system. We knew this could cause a significant delay to our entry into the States.

"I am writing to Judge Allman to tell him we are applying for Canadian visas," Paul informed me.

Paul and I had many discussions about the 'ticking clock'. There was turmoil and terror, not just for us, but for all the people of Shanghai, that worsened by the day. I was becoming very concerned for Paul's mental health.

"We don't know anyone in Canada," I said. I knew how badly Paul wanted to be reunited with his family, especially his parents. Since his father's heart attack in the DP camp in Bavaria, he often commented about how much time we really had left with our parents.

"That's very true. At least we will be in the Western Hemisphere," Paul said. "I'm asking Judge to write a letter of recommendation and a guarantee that we will have at least $3,000 on arrival. That appears to be all that is necessary to enter Canada."

The letter lay on the typewriter table unsent until the next day. After lunch I noticed a postscript, handwritten in Paul's distinctive cursive. "Held up in the office for three hours by the US Lines staff. How long do you think I can withstand this? I did not think I would have to pay with my life to enable you to escape. I hope you now realize the seriousness of the situation."

When we arrived home a week and a half later, a letter from Judge Allman was awaiting us. Enclosed in the same envelope was a copy of a letter to The Honorable Francis E. Walter of the United States House of Representatives. Paul began reading out loud. "Can you inform me of the status of H.R. 3576? I had a law firm in Shanghai which is now being liquidated by my employee, Mr. Paul A. Hoffmann. Mr. Hoffmann and his wife are Austrian citizens. By remaining behind in Shanghai, Mr. Hoffmann made it possible for myself and two other American citizens to escape the communists. Mr. and Mrs. Hoffmann were allotted Displaced Persons visa numbers under Public Law Number 555 of the 81st Congress. It is imperative that the time period for picking up visas under this law be extended. Mr. Hoffmann saved my life. I am very hopeful that by extending this time limit you will help me save both Mr. Hoffmann and his wife from the tyranny now being imposed by the Chinese communist authorities."

Paul sighed deeply as he finished reading. "At least we now know Judge Allman is taking us seriously."

"And he's asking the United States Congress to amend its laws for us. Who knew we were so important?" I said.

Paul let out a laugh for the first time in weeks. "I knew you were important. I wasn't sure about myself."

The first Friday in May 1951, I called Paul at the office around noon. I heard the receiver pick up and then slam down. The sound of metal on metal rang in my ears. I tried again with the same result. After the third attempt, I knew what needed to happen next. Paul and I had set up times during the day for me to call to check in with him to make sure he was okay. The fact that someone was picking up the phone clearly meant that there were people in the office. But what was going on? Paul's instructions to me were,"If you call and there is no answer, go to the police station and ask an officer to accompany you to the office." In the interest of time, I hailed a pedicab and in pidgin I told the driver to be quick. When we arrived at the police station, it seemed like it took forever to explain that my husband was being held prisoner in his office and I was afraid for his life. The officer brought his car around to the curb in front of the police station and together we drove to Hamilton House. We took the elevator to the second floor and I pointed to the main door of the office, which was usually open to the hallway, but on this day was closed. The police officer tried the door knob to find it locked. He pounded on the door and got no response. He pounded again and loudly shouted for whoever was in the office to open the door in both English and Chinese. After approximately five minutes we heard the bolt slide and the door opened to a dozen Chinese men standing shoulder to shoulder, arms at their sides, eyes straight ahead blocking the doorway to Paul's office. To my relief, over the heads of the employees, I saw Paul sitting at his desk, face ashen, holding his head in his hands. By now it was 5:00 p.m.

"I have been sitting here for the entire day, explaining again and again, that if I had the funds, I would pay them. Every time I have tried to get up out of my chair they have shoved me back down and accused me of lying, that I want to keep Judge Allman's money for myself, that I am an enemy of the Chinese people."

Paul's suit jacket lay rumpled on the floor. There was some swelling on the left side of his face. His necktie lay on the desk and his shirt was unbuttoned to mid chest. It was evident that he had been slapped repeatedly.

"I have had nothing to eat or drink. They haven't even let me use the bathroom," Paul said in a whisper. "They said if I was thirsty I could drink from the spittoon." (The disgusting Chinese habit of spitting still required a spittoon to be stationed conveniently wherever people gathered.)

The police officer spoke in Chinese to the man who had

unlocked the door for what seemed to be an eternity. The other employees tried to interject, but their leader would glare at them each time and they fell back into silence. Finally, the police officer turned to Paul and said, "They want you to send a telegram to Mr. Allman demanding payment of salary for the last five months." Paul picked up the phone and dialed the Western Union office.

"Send a cable to Mr. Norwood Allman, 308 Morningside Heights, New York, New York. Employees demanding immediate payment of salary. STOP. Send money now. STOP."

The police officer held the office door open and we raced down the stairs to the street. Paul gasped for air. "They said the file cabinet was just the right size for me. I thought this was the end." When we stepped to the curb, Paul clenched his stomach and vomited.

I hailed a pedicab and asked the driver to help me get Paul up off the sidewalk where he sat. His color had not improved and he seemed somewhat disoriented. When we got home to our friends' apartment Paul's heart was racing so fast, I called the doctor. The doctor arrived within the hour and administered some valerian drops. Paul fell asleep for several hours. When Paul awoke, he picked up the phone and sent another telegram to Judge Allman. It said, "Ignore previous cable STOP Details in letter to follow STOP.

Chapter Thirty
Danger, Dilemma and Despair
Shanghai June 1951

Finally in June the licenses came through and a new flurry of activity began. Clients were emerging from the woodwork, making claims that were often unsubstantiated. Somehow, Paul was now held responsible for everyone's problems. The Chinese government continued to set up insurmountable roadblocks. Paul turned his attention to shutting down the offices of Allman, Kops and Lee. Government officials had locked file cabinets and Judge Allman's desk, so he no longer had access to the written information to prove terms of agreement. He had to rely on what he remembered or what Judge Allman wrote in his letters.

And still no word on our exit visas. As claim after claim surfaced, the Chinese government refused to issue our visas until all accounts had been settled.

Our lives were consumed by letter writing. There was not a day that I did not hear the clacking of the keys of the old manual Royal typewriter after dinner each night, or for a good portion of the day on weekends. The smell of typewriter oil infused the small apartment that we were sharing with the Vilenskys. The box of onion skin paper to the left of the typewriter table emptied rapidly as the file folder to the right filled with carbon copies of every letter. Paul's legal training told him that he needed to document his every word. He knew that it may be important in the future to remind others of what was said or done. He kept copies of all his business correspondence, often written at home to be far from the roving eyes of the increasingly disgruntled employees, still waiting to be paid as Paul dealt with entangled termination agreements. Every step, every decision, every action required lengthy explanations to Judge Allman. The family missives were sometimes copied as well. That way he wouldn't have to repeat himself when sending letters to his parents, and then to his sister in Boston. When writing to Licci, more often than not he would instruct her to forward his letter to his parents in an effort to save both time and postage.

As demanding, draining and overwhelming the task of letter writing had become, it held a dim candle to the emotional toll and impact receiving letters had on us. The mail system was far from efficient. Letters we received had likely been air mailed to Russia, arriving in Beijing, then transported by train to Shanghai. Often letters were delayed for several weeks and more recent letters would arrive before letters that had been posted two to three weeks earlier. We felt like we were piecing together a puzzle to figure out the timeline of events.

When we arrived home from work, our very first task was to check the small wooden carved table near the door where the house boy would leave the letters that arrived that day.

Sometimes two weeks would go by without any word of family. Paul's anxiety was palpable as we awaited word of his parents endless journey across the Pacific Ocean, between the continents of North and South America through the Panama Canal, across the Atlantic Ocean, through Europe by train to

Southern Germany, only to board a ship again to finally arrive in New York City, eventually settling in the small city of Utica, New York. Paul's cousin Fred, one of two of Paul's family members who was able to make it to the States at the beginning of the War, had found a position for Oskar at a state psychiatric hospital in upstate New York. Even though Oskar was a dermatologist, not a psychiatrist, doctors of all specialties were needed. All that was required was proof of completion of medical school prior to World War I and the passing of the GED, Graduate Equivalency Degree, exam in English, which Oskar did with flying colors. But before Lili and Oskar were settled in Utica there was an entire year filled with worry; crowded conditions, seasickness, dental problems, financial woes, and by the time they were settled in the DP camp, Oskar had suffered a heart attack. Not only were their letters filled with their struggles, there was the constant concern about us. When would we be able to leave? Were we safe? By September, I was pregnant. Was I healthy? Would I be able to travel?

Sometimes, Paul could hardly eat his dinner after reading one of these letters. No sooner than the last morsel had passed his lips, he would be back at the typewriter, doing his best to allay his parents' fears and shore them up for the next episode in their saga. By the time he was done, he collapsed on the bed utterly exhausted for a restless night's sleep.

Chapter Thirty-One
Liquidation
Shanghai July 1951

On July 10,1951 an auction was held to liquidate the contents of suite 208 Hamilton House, the offices of Allman, Kops and Lee. Books and papers that Judge knew he wanted were boxed, ready for shipping to the States. Lawyers from other firms stopped by to peruse Judge's books and some were purchased. Paul was pleased with any cash he could accumulate, no matter the amount. Files that contained information relevant to Chinese firms were also boxed and I had arranged for my cousin to send the truck from the fur store to take them to the godown. Over three days, Paul dictated as I typed another letter to Judge Allman, four pages single-spaced containing twenty-two bullet points updating the status of individuals, accounts, claims, assets and actions. I was in total awe of how Paul kept all the details of each situation organized in his head. Now that the office staff had received their final severance, Paul was office manager, accountant, and typist. I jumped in wherever I could to lighten his load by taking dictation and re-typing agreements. Paul kept Peter on staff knowing he would be lost without him.

Once again Paul restarted the process of applying for exit visas. Paperwork verifying that claims had been settled had to be generated. The Chinese government agencies were in no rush. All we could do was ask Peter to make a phone call or visit the police station responsible for issuing the visas every few days to check on the status of our applications. Paul asked Judge Allman to issue a Power of Attorney to another Austrian citizen, A.J. Hajek, a friend of his parents who appeared to be in no rush to return to Austria, to manage whatever affairs remained for AKL. This would make Mr. Hajek the responsible party and be essential if we were to receive our exit visas.

On July 31, 1951, at 5:00 p.m. Paul locked the doors of 208 Hamilton House for the very last time.

When Paul arrived home that evening, I could see the dejection not only on his face, but throughout his entire body. There was no more car, no more chauffeur. We each either took a trolley or pedicab to return home from work each evening. Paul kicked off his shoes, threw his suit jacket over the back of a chair and lay down, stretching out the full length of the couch.

"What a rush it was five years ago when I started my career at AKL, just one year after the War was over. I had completed my university studies and was immediately hired by one of the most prestigious law firms in Shanghai. I can't believe who I have brushed shoulders with: representatives of General Motors, Standard Oil, General Electric, DuPont, not to mention the Flying Tigers and innumerable Chinese companies. We had comforts I didn't think were possible in China, especially for refugees. In the past two years Judge Allman's law practice, which had been in Shanghai since 1924, has been reduced to a sealed desk, some locked file cabinets, and a few boxes in a godown on the Whangpoo River bank. It was a fairytale, a dream come true that has disappeared in a puff of smoke."

SHALAMA

I sat down next to Paul on the couch and just listened. Every part of his body revealed his disappointment. He spoke softly. His voice sounded weak.

"While there is any work to attend to, in the mornings I'll be going to Hajek's office on Yuen Ming Yuen Road. The sealed files and Judge's desk have been sent there," he said.

"At least now you can focus your attention on obtaining our exit visas," I responded, trying to sound hopeful.

"I wish it were that simple. A business acquaintance applied three months ago. When he asked the Controller about his status, the Controller asked him how long he had been in China. He replied, "thirty-one years". The Controller's response was, "Then you may wait a little longer." The word on the street is that for foreigners with no business connections, the wait for an exit visa is two months. For people like us it is at least four months. We really need Judge Allman to issue Hajek that POA if we are going to get out of here anytime soon."

"I have complete faith that Judge Allman will come through, as promised." That is what I said out loud. After all these months, I'm not sure that I believed my own words.

Chapter Thirty-Two
Vicious Cycle
Shanghai August 1951

Although the offices of AKL were now closed and the licenses for the remittance of salaries had been issued, additional claims continued to emerge. Just when Paul thought he had shut the door on another client, a new claim would surface. Most often it was a landlord looking for past rent.

We watched as those with no business ties were granted visas and were able to leave. We also saw those who challenged claims and lost in court ended up in jail. Paul brought this to Judge Allman's attention in every letter. Clearly, jail in Shanghai was not an option to be considered under any circumstance. Judge made repeated appeals to the Federal Reserve Bank in New York City to extend the existing licenses. The head of the Foreign Assets Control refused to extend the license without a guarantee from the Chinese authorities that we would be issued exit visas. Paul begged Judge Allman to explain to the powers that be that they could not dictate the actions of a sovereign nation. Judge began to see our predicament and encouraged Paul to do whatever was necessary to settle remaining claims. Paul felt that we would be able to apply for our exit visa the moment he handed over all the payoffs because the manager of the President Lines, who had an identical situation, had finally received his exit permit.

The best news of the summer was that Paul's parents, Lili and Oskar, had arrived in New York City on August 31, 1951 and were on their way to Boston to be reunited with Licci and her family. Paul handed me the telegram from his parents when I arrived home that evening.

"This is wonderful news!" I said as I gave him a hug.

"Yes, I could not be happier for them. Three quarters of the family is now where they should be; my family in the States and yours in Israel. That leaves us, still blowing in the wind. What an entangled mess! Everyday, I wake up thinking reason will prevail and we will be on our way. I don't know what else to do. This letter writing campaign has us stuck in a vicious cycle of bureaucracy."

"I know you are doing everything you can. One thing is for certain, we can never give up. Coming to China, surviving the War, finishing school... it's not like anything has been particularly easy for you. Why start now?"

Once again, I brought a small smile, but a smile nonetheless, to my husband's face. Once again that was all I could do.

Chapter Thirty-Three
NEWS
Shanghai September 1951

How can a single day bring both tremendous joy and unbearable sorrow? We arrived home a little earlier than usual on September 30,1951, hoping to take a walk before dinner as the weather had turned dry and cool, a welcome relief from the oppressive summer heat and humidity that seemed to hang over Shanghai even a little bit longer than usual that year. Finally, the servants could stop their daily routine of wiping down the shoes and anything made of leather to avoid them becoming moldy. Paul did not have to change both shirt and tie at lunch time now. During the summer months, he would watch the pools of perspiration form where his elbows rested on the desk as he worked. His necktie, very much a requirement for professional dress, would be soaked from neck to tip by noon. Even a short nap resulted in our bed linens being soaked through.

There on the wooden table adjacent to the front door were two blue airmail letters, one from Paul's sister in Boston and one from my brother in Israel. We grabbed our respective letters and dropped down onto the couch next to each other eagerly and carefully opening our letters like two children on Christmas morning. Once again, it had been more than two weeks since we had word from either family, I saw a smile spread across Paul's face as he read the news of his brother-in law's new job, his nephew's success in math in first grade, and the warm hospitality the Praegers were enjoying with family and friends in Boston.

And I could not catch my breath as I read the contents of Teva's missive. As if lack of food and difficult living conditions were not enough of a challenge in Israel, my father had not been feeling well. "Papa has exhibited a variety of gastrointestinal symptoms over the last several weeks that have caused him considerable discomfort," Teva wrote. "He finally agreed to go to the doctor the first week in September and the doctor scheduled an exploratory surgery. The news is not good. An operation was performed on September 14. The doctor was hoping he would be able to remove whatever was causing Papa's distress. Unfortunately, this was not the case. Upon examination, the doctor saw such extensive stomach cancer that had spread to the surrounding organs that he sutured the incision and said there was nothing more that could be done."

My head fell back onto the headrest of the couch. Paul, jarred out of his own reverie, asked "What's wrong?" I could not speak and handed him Teva's letter to read for himself.

"How unfair!" How incredibly unfair," I sobbed. "He waited an entire lifetime to enter the Promised Land. This was the year to celebrate Passover in Jerusalem. He worked so hard to live his dream."

Papa never stopped believing Israel would grow and prosper and provide a safe haven for Jews from all over the world, especially now after the devastation from the Holocaust. After such a catastrophic tragedy, how had the Jewish people rallied their strength to create a new nation in the middle of the desert?

Where did they find their strength? Now it was a reality, and Papa was not going to be able to see what was possible, what the future would hold. I looked at Paul as tears rolled down my face. He held me close as we sat there in silence as the sun set in the western sky, casting long dark shadows into the room. "Will I ever see Papa again?" I asked.

Chapter Thirty-Four
Papa
Shanghai November 1951

"I had intended this letter to be Licci's birthday letter," Paul said out loud for my benefit as he began typing the weekly letter to his family. "Unfortunately, I must start with very sad news. We received a telegram early yesterday morning that Shirley's father passed away on the 21st of November."

I sat in the red floral overstuffed armchair where I usually did my knitting, listening to the too familiar clatter of the typewriter keys. Today the yarn and needles were weights in my hands and I finally gave up. The unfinished socks, intended for Paul, lay in my lap. Just two days earlier I had received a handwritten letter from Papa telling me his health was improving. He wrote that the news that I was pregnant was the best medicine. I had closed my eyes and imagined his hug as we shared the joy and anticipation of his first grandchild. I so hoped by sharing our good news, by some miracle, he would live to see our baby. It was Saturday, so technically we were not sitting shivah, but the few friends and neighbors still left in Shanghai continued to stop by throughout the day to pay their respects. We telegraphed

Mama and Teva and followed up immediately with a letter, which felt so insignificant, but was all we could do. I imagined Mama and Teva, clinging to each other graveside as Papa was lowered into the ground wrapped in a white linen shroud. In the dry desert of Israel, the commandment of 'dust to dust' could be followed. Paul thought I was very brave the way I handled the news of my father's passing. My heart ached in a way that defied explanation. How does one express a pain that deep? Before Paul, I could not fathom a greater love than the love my father shared with me.

Chapter Thirty-Five
Down to the Wire
Shanghai December 1951

The dreary damp early weeks of December continued to be filled with news of unfulfilled promises and negotiations. The Foreign Affairs Bureau continued to wield its weight and Paul showed tremendous forbearance as he attempted to negotiate settlements that were hopefully going to bring us closer to being able to leave Shanghai.

We were buoyed by the fact that I was now through the first trimester of my pregnancy and was feeling fine. I visited the doctor about every three weeks and he assured us everything was going as well as expected. The letters from the relatives from abroad had begun to suggest that I leave Shanghai ahead of Paul. The doctor did not seem to think this was necessary.

"I am not leaving here without you," I told Paul as we left Dr. Li's office after my check-up during the first week in December.

"I agree," said Paul. "There are just too many unknowns right now and it would drive me crazy not knowing where you were or how you were everyday. We need to be together so I will be there to help if something goes wrong."

"Nothing is going to go wrong. You heard the doctor. This baby is going to be born in America, the first born American in our family. I am more concerned about leaving you here in Shanghai to fend for yourself. There are still a lot of good looking women here."

"Oh, is that so?" Paul chuckled. "What makes you think I would be interested in anyone but you?"

"Your reputation precedes you, you know," I said, giving him a coy smile.

"But that was all before you," he said, patting my hand as we walked down the street, our arms intertwined.

Finally, by December 15th the money to pay the last claim arrived. When Paul came home with this news, we danced around the table, poured a glass of wine and toasted to our departure from Shanghai. Was it true? Were we finally on the way out to begin the rest of our lives? To rejoin family and friends and to start our own family in a free country? After all these months, it was surreal and too much to digest all at once.

The next day Paul went to the police station to apply for our exit visas from Shanghai. The lines were becoming shorter as there were so few of us left. He had already started the process for exit visas from Hong Kong and English transit visas in case we would travel on an English ship. There were still so many unknowns and every step was contingent on what happened prior. Paul had written to his cousin, Erich, a doctor in London who escaped Vienna in 1938, to ask if we might stay with him and his wife if we ended up having to go to England. Our housemates, David and family, were now in England and would soon be on their way to New York. Although we appreciated our privacy, we were somewhat lonely, and more than a little bit jealous.

"I can't believe David will see my parents before I do. Since

SHALAMA

David saw us just before his departure, my parents will have an eye witness report that we are well and have been truthful in our reporting. I am a little hopeful today that we will have our exit visas by the middle of February."

Even though so many of the claims had been settled, and others in positions similar to Paul's had been released from their obligations and had been issued exit visas, we both knew we could not be overly enthusiastic. The instances we had begun making plans for our departure, only to accept additional delays, had become too many to count. We sat down to dinner that evening in silence. The evening street sounds of Shanghai permeated the air and became our background music as it floated in on the fluttering curtains of the open windows.

CHAPTER THIRTY-SIX
Lost in Thought
Connecticut 2003

"Amma?"

Shalama had become quiet and was gazing off into the distance.

"Are you tired?" asked Cara. "Maybe we should finish this tomorrow?"

"No, no, no," asserted Shalama. "Who knows what tomorrow brings. We only know we have today. We only know we have this minute. Let's get this done. Time is a gift not to be wasted."

"Those months of waiting in Shanghai taught you that?"

"Absolutely! Your grandfather knew exactly what he had to do to get us out of Shanghai, yet we were sure of nothing. I know Papa can seem impatient at times. That may be because his reservoir of patience was almost completely drained dry during those couple of years when we were stuck in Shanghai. My pregnancy had created a new urgency. If we didn't leave soon, or the baby came early, we might not be able to travel for another six months, or maybe even a year. We only had my salary to live on and I wouldn't be able to work; we had no other source of income. The communists kept changing the rules. What restrictions might they impose next that could further delay our departure? Even *worse, they might devise some trumped-up charges against Papa to try to squeeze more money out of the 'Capitalist running dog', or send him to prison."*

"How did you maintain your focus?" asked Cara.

"The baby. We had to make it out safely for the baby."

Chapter Thirty-Seven
Now What?
Shanghai January 1952

Apparently, we weren't the only ones sitting on pins and needles, wondering when we would finally be able to leave Shanghai. Judge's first letter of the New Year began with, "What is the status of your exit visas? The Treasury is threatening to cancel all licenses unless you are granted an exit visa! I'm putting up a hell of a fight! Everything will be all mucked up again, if you're not out of there soon."

"I guess we're important again," Paul said with resignation as he read the letter. "It would be nice if Judge could define 'soon' so I could pass it on to the authorities here.

My emotions had begun to mirror Paul's. I knew exactly how he felt. It seemed like the issuing of exit visas was getting more and more random. Some were granted visas without having fully liquidated, while others had complied with every directive that the Foreign Affairs Bureau required and were still waiting. Mr. Hajek, the Austrian who was now the proxy manager for AKL, was called to the FAB and was told he had to present his curriculum vitae if Paul was going to receive an exit visa.

SHALAMA

"At least it shows that they are handling our paperwork," Paul told me.

On January 16, a cable arrived. Paul had been looking out the window when he saw the delivery boy hop off his bicycle.

"Mr. Hoffmann, Mr. Hoffmann," he heard the boy cry out and he ran down the two flights of stairs. Paul placed five yuan in the boy's hand and quickly returned to the apartment.

"It's from US Lines," Paul said. "Passage has been confirmed for you and your wife on Messageries Maritime Liner *Felix Roussel* departing Hong Kong March 7, 1952 arriving Marseille April 7, 1952."

"That's incredibly good news!" I gushed.

"It will be," Paul responded, "when we get our exit visas. As of today, we are not going anywhere."

Chapter Thirty-Eight
Saturday Blues
Shanghai February 1952

Saturdays determined what kind of week it would be for us. Paul rose early and walked to the corner to pick up a newspaper. Each Saturday, a list of exit visas that had been issued that week was published in the paper. On February 2, 1952 Paul wrote to his parents: "If you look at the calendar, you will see that today is Saturday and I am affected by the *Saturday Blues*, a sickness which only befalls foreigners, and only in Shanghai. As you can guess, we have not received our visas again. I know it is foolish to be impatient. Impatience will do nothing to move this process along, but who can blame me? If we don't get the visas until February 16 we cannot reach the ship on time, and will have to consider flying, which I don't think is a good idea for Shirley in her condition. It's also more expensive and we will only be able to take one suitcase of clothing. If the visa doesn't come through until mid-March, we will have to stay here until the birth of the baby."

My due date was May 15, 1952, which still sounded far away, but really it wasn't. Once we were allowed to leave Shanghai, we would have to travel by train to Canton, a trip that used to take no more than a day. Under communist control, we had heard that it was not unusual for this trip to be unreasonably slow due to all the security checks along the way. Then Paul hoped to have several days in Hong Kong to complete some business for AKL before we were on our way to Europe. If we made the scheduled departure on the *Felix Rousell* on March 7, then we were in transit for another thirty days before arriving in Marseille. Our fingers were crossed that Messageries Maritime Lines had been successful in arranging for a doctor to be on this voyage. They had informed us, due to my condition, I would not be allowed to make the trip unless there was a doctor on board. If we were lucky, we would find a place in Europe to await the arrival of our baby by sometime in mid-April. But our first task when we arrived in Europe was to check on the status of our immigration papers to the States. We were told that the visa division was in Milan, Italy and we would have to register in person. We had no arrangements for housing, doctors or hospitals and it was clear now that this baby was not going to be born in America. We had run out of time. All of a sudden May 15 was around the corner.

Despite the worry, I couldn't help but be excited about our upcoming adventure. All I knew was China, and only two cities Harbin and Shanghai, within the vast landscape. Movies, books and, of course, *Life Magazine,* the incredible photo journal, had been my introduction to the world beyond. If we reached the *Felix Roussel* for departure on March 7, 1952 from Hong Kong we would arrive in Manila two days later. The next ports of call would be Saigon, Singapore, then Colombo and Djibouti. We'd travel through the Suez Canal to Port Said. April 7 was our scheduled arrival in Marseille. I couldn't wait to buy lovely baby clothes in Hong Kong. And what other trinkets and lovely things would we find in all those ports of call? We would be able to disembark and explore at each stop. I just could not wait. The days began to pass quickly.

The morning of Saturday, February 9, 1952, arrived damp and raw. The temperature hovered around freezing and mothlike snowflakes fluttered down from the sky. We no longer had a house boy to run errands.

I turned to Paul and said, "I'll go down to see if the shopkeeper's boy will go buy the newspaper for us today. I'm sure he'll appreciate a few extra yuan."

The child returned in less than ten minutes. "Missy, your paper," he said.

Paul was seated at the kitchen table. I handed him the paper and he quickly opened it to page three, the page where the list of exit visas appeared each week. His eyes quickly scrolled down the list of names. He dropped the paper on the table and his face fell into his hands. At first, I did not know how to interpret what had just happened. Was the news good or bad? The window of opportunity was closing on us. If we did not receive our visas this week there was a very good chance we would not make it to Hong Kong in time to depart on the *Felix Roussel*. Paul turned to look up at me. Tears were running down his face. "Thank God!" he said. He pointed to the second column of names. At the very top I saw our names, one above the other:

Paul A. Hoffmann

Shulamis Froloff Hoffmann

We were on the list. We were leaving Shanghai.

Chapter Thirty-Nine
Free at Last?
Shanghai February 1952

The phone did not stop ringing all day Saturday and well into Sunday. Friends, acquaintances, business associates, all wanted to congratulate us and wish us well. Every time I thought I could sit down and rest for a few moments, the phone would ring again. Paul and I started taking turns fielding the calls. The hardest ones to take were from those who were still waiting to hear about their own visas. Between their kind words we heard the disappointment that they were still not among the Chosen. Their Exodus would have to wait.

Immediately after seeing our names on the list, Paul ran into the bedroom to get dressed. He put on his coat, pulled a knit cap over his ears and wrapped a scarf around his neck. "I shouldn't be gone too long," he said. "I'm going to the train station to purchase our tickets to Hong Kong."

"Voila!" Paul said when he returned. "Train tickets to Hong Kong via Canton for Monday, February 25. That should get us to Hong Kong in plenty of time for me to wrap up business for AKL and for you to shop for the baby before we leave for Europe. I can't believe I will be returning to Europe. It's been more than thirteen years since I arrived in Shanghai."

"And it has been twelve years since my family arrived in

Shanghai," I said. "We both really have only lived in two places in our lives; you in Vienna and Shanghai, and me in Harbin and Shanghai. Our worlds were so different, so far apart, yet Shanghai brought us, and so many others together. There really was a certain magic in this amazing city."

"There is so much that we will miss. But Shanghai will never be the Shanghai we knew. It's best if we take our good memories with us and try to forget some of the horrors we have witnessed in the last two years," Paul said. "We will have plenty of time to reminisce once we are safely sailing the Pacific and Indian Oceans. I know we have been very prepared, but there will be plenty to do in the coming days." I could see the to-do lists forming in Paul's head. "I have to go to the police station on Tuesday to pick up the visas. Hopefully, things will go smoothly and the day won't be wasted. I'll go first thing in the morning and try to catch the officials while they are still fresh and in good moods."

"I will have to give my notice at the Gas Company on Monday. The Kadoories have had to turn control of the company over to the Chinese. They will be happy to give my job to a loyal Party member. Friday will have to be my last day. That will give us one week to tie up all the loose ends."

By Sunday evening, after all the letters had been posted to inform Paul's family and Judge Allman that we had finally been granted permission to leave Shanghai, that we were leaving China, we again collapsed on our bed and fell into a deep sleep.

We awoke Monday morning to the sun shining brightly through the east facing windows. All that was left of the previous day's snow was a few small puddles on sidewalks and streets. We had to remind ourselves that the beautiful weather could not disguise what Shanghai had become. Shanghai, the 'Paris of the East', was no more and we were leaving because we had no choice. We were no longer welcome.

At the close of business on Friday, February 15, 1952, Paul was waiting curbside with a pedicab as I emerged from the Shanghai Gas Company for the last time, weighed down with several bouquets of flowers. The office staff had arranged a lovely send-off luncheon for their last foreign employee. For almost eight years, thanks to Morris, I had worked side by side with my Chinese co-workers taking home a decent salary. I was one of six female employees among the staff of more than sixty mostly Chinese men. While the ambiance in the office itself hadn't changed much, when leaving the office each day, I walked alone. There were no expressions of farewell, not even eye contact, once we were on the street. It was as if I had become invisible. Paul said the same thing happened in Vienna within hours, if not minutes, of the Anschluss, when Hitler marched his troops into Austria. Friends were no longer friends.

I understood that my colleagues had good reason to be afraid of being associated with me. It was no secret that my husband was often seen at the Foreign Affairs Bureau and court, not to mention the police station. Everyone knew someone who had been the victim of one of the peoples' public trials. While there was no doubt that the expressions of regret on my leaving from most of my co-workers were sincere, there also was an underlying sense of relief, for both my friends and me. For more than two years now, we could feel the overriding tension in the air. Anything that relieved that tension was appreciated.

Paul took the flowers out of my hands as he offered his other hand to assist me as I hoisted myself into the pedicab. My growing belly was always in the way now. I found myself twisting and bending in very unusual ways as I maneuvered through the day.

"I'm glad this is your last day of work," Paul said. "I have been trying all day to do our packing, but the phone calls and correspondence related to AKL business just won't stop. Can you believe that I had a query from Buenos Aires this morning about registering a trademark here in China? Don't they read the newspaper? I had to stop to respond and explain the situation. They are going to learn soon enough that they are not going to want to do business in China under the communists. In other news, Judge Allman has sent an affidavit to the consulate in Hong Kong to support our visa applications to the States. He asked the Hong Kong representatives of the two shipping lines that were clients to do the same. He wants to impress upon the Consul that three American lives, Paul Kops, Mrs. Allman and himself, were saved by my remaining behind to settle accounts for several American businesses. He seems to think we might be able to come to the States directly from Hong Kong if the right people intervene. That's optimistic thinking on his part, but I guess it doesn't hurt to try."

"I also wrote to my parents telling them, hopefully, this is the last letter from Shanghai," Paul added. "I don't want to be bogged down with letter writing over the next few days if we can avoid it."

I just listened as the pedicab took us home to the French Concession. The pictures of Uncle Singaus navigating his truck through the streets of Shanghai the day I arrived from Harbin with Mama, Papa and Teva were fresh in my mind. All that was new and surprising that day, was familiar now. For twelve years, Shanghai was home. In ten days we would be homeless.

Chapter Forty
Final Hours
Shanghai February 1952

The morning of February 25, 1952 was a blur. I do remember that the weather was somewhat chilly because I can see our winter coats lying across the two suitcases that were packed and ready to go by the door of the apartment. All that we would be taking with us was the clothing for our one month trip to Europe. Everything else that we owned had been shipped to Paul's parents and was in a storage facility in New York City waiting for our eventual arrival. Paul carried a briefcase with all our documents, a book to read and a deck of playing cards. I had a large purse which included a small knitting project, a sweater for the baby, to fill the sixty hours we would end up spending on the train to Canton. The communist authorities allowed for twenty ounces of silver and two ounces of gold to be taken out of the country. All the silver that we had received as wedding presents was packed away in the shipping containers that were on their way to New York. My beautiful bamboo-shaped gold bracelet weighed more than two ounces so I went to the jeweler the previous Friday and had a link removed and sold the gold back to him. Paul wore his gold signet ring that had left Vienna with him and carried his grandfather's gold pocket watch in his vest pocket with the gold chain clipped to a belt loop of his pants.

Thursday afternoon before our scheduled departure, my school friend Mary stopped by the apartment. She had married an Englishman and they were still awaiting exit visas to England.

We spoke briefly about the weather and our upcoming journey. Then Mary opened her purse and placed a velvet jewelry box in the middle of the table. "Can I ask you a favor?" she said.

"I'll help if I can," I replied.

Mary opened the box and two pieces of exquisite jewelry lay inside. One was a seven-carat diamond ring in a platinum setting. The other was a brooch encrusted with probably twenty diamonds of all sizes.

"Will you take this with you when you leave on Monday? I've heard the border guards do not pay attention to the jewelry that you are wearing." She slipped the ring onto the ring finger of my right hand. "Pack the brooch in among your toiletries. Hopefully, the guards won't notice it." She opened her purse again, pulled out a business card and handed it to me. "When you get to Hong Kong, call this number. Someone will come to your hotel to pick it up."

"Can't you do the same thing and take this with you when you leave? What if the guards confiscate these pieces?" I asked.

"I have a number of other pieces of jewelry I hope to take with me. It will definitely draw attention if I have several items like this. If they confiscate them, so be it. It's a risk I'm willing to take. With the value of the currency right now, it's not worth trying to sell."

Paul had been out running errands and returned shortly after Mary had left. His eyes widened when he saw the humongous gemstone on my finger. In contrast my engagement ring, although a perfect stone, was less than one carat.

"Where did that come from?" he asked in surprise. I repeated my conversation with Mary. "I guess there is minimal risk to us. If the pieces get confiscated, they get confiscated," Paul said.

At 9:30 a.m. on February 25 we heard a car horn. Peter Chang had arranged for a taxi and would be accompanying us to the train station. Once again, dependable Peter was there by our side to ensure our safety. Of all our friends and acquaintances, Peter was with us until the end. He was the only one brave enough to see us to the train. Even Jerry Liu, who attended Aurora University with Paul, and for whom Paul secured a position at AKL, sent a note with a small departure gift, saying it was too dangerous to see us off. He was afraid to be seen with foreigners.

The last few days before our departure were harrowing. When the phone rang, we could not help but startle. There were threats to Paul's life and attempts at blackmail. Paul would answer the phone and listen for a moment or two. As soon as he was able to ascertain the nature of the call, that it was not relevant to our departure, he hung up.

"Just another crook trying to squeeze another dollar out of me before we leave," he would say. Paul did his best to maintain a calm demeanor. I knew this was just an act, as much to spare me as to try to control his own fear. Once or twice I saw him run to the bathroom after he hung up the phone. Through the closed door, I heard him wretch into the toilet. We received word from Mr. Hajek when we arrived in Vienna two months later, that in fact the police had come to arrest Paul shortly after we left for the train station on the morning of February 25. Apparently, the charge was espionage. Paul had worked with a Chinese lawyer, a Dr. Ai, to translate some published legal decrees that were forwarded to Judge Allman. Judge needed this information in order to advise clients in the States on legal problems in China.

The day after we left, Dr. Ai was arrested and disappeared. Even with the best efforts of Judge's contacts we never learned Dr. Ai's fate. The Reign of Terror was in full throttle by the time we left Shanghai and one can only imagine the brutality the poor man suffered.

When we arrived at the train station the taxi driver and Peter placed our suitcases on the sidewalk. Paul took Peter's hand and held it in a firm handshake.

"You better leave us here, Peter. I don't want you to risk any more than you already have. I will never be able to thank you enough for all that you have done over the past two years. You are incredibly brave and have more integrity than any man I have ever known."

These were the last words Paul would have with Peter. We knew that any attempts to contact him subsequent to our leaving could have devastating results. Just like Dr. Ai, and all that was dear to us in Shanghai, he was lost to us forever.

Paul signaled to a porter to help us with our suitcases and we proceeded to the platform.

Chapter Forty-One
Prisoners on a Train
Shanghai to Canton February 25-28, 1952

At the top of the stairs to the platform stood two stern uniformed Chinese custom officials. They signaled the porter to place the suitcases in front of them, flicked the latches open and dumped the entire contents of the suitcases on the dusty platform. After rummaging through our clothing and finding nothing of interest, the official ordered the porter to move our suitcases to the side so the next set of passengers could be subject to the same humiliation. As the porter shoved our clothing and luggage away from where the guards were standing, a glint of something shiny in the pile of dirt under my suitcase caught my eye. I leaned down over my heavy belly to take a look and quickly realized it was Mary's brooch. Either the custom's official had totally missed it, or assumed it was a garish piece of costume jewelry. After all, who would be stupid enough to put a valuable piece of jewelry in their luggage in plain view? Clearly in my haste to pack, I had been careless in placing the brooch out of sight. I hurriedly bent down and shoved the brooch in my coat pocket. When I felt certain no one was looking, I found the zipper pouch with my toiletries and quickly rammed the brooch to the bottom of the bag under my makeup and anti-nausea medications. I placed the pouch in the bottom corner of the suitcase and piled the mess of clothing that had been so neatly folded the night before tightly around it. This was the first of five times that our luggage would be searched; each time everything in the suitcases was thrown on the ground, contents left in disarray. Each time, somehow, the guards missed the brooch.

When we finally boarded the train we were locked into our first class sleeper compartment. A Chinese soldier patrolled the corridor between the compartments. There was a dining car on the train but we were not allowed to use it. Fortunately, food was brought to the compartment because we had not thought to bring any with us. If we needed to use the bathroom, we knocked on the door and waited for the soldier to acknowledge the knock. He would unlock the door and watch us stagger to the end of the car, trying not to lose our balance as the train jerked in response to the aging tracks.

On one of these trips to the bathroom the guard had looked into our compartment and saw the deck of playing cards on the table that folded down between the facing bench seats. We had been playing gin rummy. Upon my return, the guard smiled, pointed to his chest and then to the cards on the foldout table between Paul and me.

" I think he wants to play with us," I said to Paul.

"We can try," Paul replied. He motioned for the soldier to sit beside him. The soldier propped the compartment door open with my valise and slid onto the brown leather bench seat next to Paul. Paul dealt us each ten cards. He showed the soldier his cards and attempted to demonstrate the necessary groupings of cards. The soldier smiled and nodded, appearing to make sense of what Paul had shown him. After two hands, it was clear that the soldier had no idea as to the rules of the game, presenting unexpected combinations of cards. When Paul attempted to rearrange the cards on the table in an effort to demonstrate the correct groupings again, the soldier blurted out something in angry-sounding Chinese, stood up abruptly without the least attempt to disguise his frustration, and slammed the compartment door behind him as he left.

'What do you think he said?" I asked Paul.

"It would be nice if he said, 'Thank you, but no thank you'. Don't think he was anywhere near that polite," Paul replied as he scooped up the cards and shuffled the deck.

We both giggled as Paul dealt the cards again, this time just for the two of us.

Chapter Forty-Two
A Brief Sojourn
Canton February 27, 1952

It was early morning when the train pulled into the station in Canton. The skies were overcast and the air felt heavy and humid. We dragged our suitcases down from the overhead racks.

"My goodness, Paul Hoffmann, you do look a mess. Did you sleep at all last night?" I asked my exhausted husband, trying to sound lighthearted. The dark circles under his eyes answered my question.

"Be glad you are not entering a beauty contest today. I don't think there is a prize for very pregnant women in unwashed rumpled clothing who haven't bathed in three days," was Paul's glib retort.

I could not deny that he was right. An abundance of cologne had been used by the passengers that morning in an attempt to disguise the pungent odors that wafted throughout the train; a condition that we were guilty of contributing to as well. My hair was pulled back tightly against my head with combs and I had not bothered to apply any lipstick or rouge. The top three buttons of Paul's shirt were unbuttoned and his jacket was draped over his left forearm. Perspiration was already visible on his forehead and temples. The weather in Canton was warmer than what we had left behind in Shanghai.

We stepped out onto the platform and there, once again, were the soldiers waiting to inspect our luggage. This struck us as totally absurd as no one had been allowed to board the train at any of the inspection stops, nor were we allowed out of our compartment. Although we knew there were other foreigners on the train, we had only seen them on the platform in Shanghai. The only other person we saw on our sixty-hour journey was the soldier who had asked to play cards with us. We knew better than to object and placed the suitcases in front of the soldiers and I held my breath as I watched our clothing and personal belongings tumble to the ground onto the dusty, dirty platform. This time the toiletries pouch remained shut. By now every last piece of clothing was rumpled and dirty. Once again we hurried to scoop everything back into the suitcases. I would try to repack when we arrived at the hotel.

A bus was waiting to take us to the police station to register our arrival. From the police station we were taken to a hotel to spend the night before boarding another train for a three-hour trip to Hong Kong.

I was exhausted and could not wait to arrive at the hotel, anticipating a bath and a change of clothes. On the half-hour ride to the hotel both Paul and I stared out the window, not speaking. He took my hand and placed it in his lap, gently resting his hand on mine.

Canton, on the east bank of the Pearl River, like most cities in China, was a glorious mix of old and new. At the base of the gentle hills were multi-story apartment buildings. Fishermen wearing round, broad flat-brimmed hats perched on the top of their heads, guided their canopied flatboats down the river wielding large oars almost the length of the boat themselves. In the streets groups of men and women could be seen hauling heavy carts, thick ropes slung over their shoulders, while others were raking trash into heaps off to the side of the road. A young man, a long pole slung across his shoulders, with large buckets of water at each end trudged up the hill. In the distance stood the tall conical Flowery Pagoda, peeking out between the apartment buildings below. I never tired of the scenes of day-to-day life in China. The blatant contrasts were a constant reminder of the inherent flaws in Chinese society, yet the accomplishments of this diverse, hard-working culture could not be denied.

At the police station we were given strict instructions that we were not to leave the hotel until the next morning when we would be picked up for the last leg of our trip to Hong Kong. The hotel was a five-story rectangular pagoda-shaped building. Thankfully, bellmen were waiting at the door to assist with our luggage. I took a seat in a high backed carved wooden chair in the lobby as Paul approached the registration desk to obtain our room key. As I sat there mindlessly, I looked down at my hands, then my legs and feet. For the first time in my pregnancy I noticed the swelling in my extremities. I guess the heat and the prolonged sitting on the train had taken its toll. I knew that swelling was common in late pregnancy, especially in warm weather, so I didn't feel overly concerned. I tried to spin the seven carat diamond ring that had easily slipped onto the ring finger of my right hand just a week earlier. Now it would hardly move.

Paul signaled me from across the lobby to join him by holding up the room key. With considerable effort I pushed up out of the chair and waddled across the lobby. Paul watched me with concern.

"Are you okay?" he asked. "There is no elevator and they've

given us a room on the third floor."

"Just stiff," I replied. Leaving Shanghai was just the first step. Paul was clearly still hyper-vigilant and I didn't want to add to his concern by pointing out what I had noticed about my condition. "You walk ahead. I'll see you at the top."

By the time I reached the top of the stairs Paul had already opened the door to room 302, allowing the bellman to place our suitcases at the foot of the bed. The room was shabby. Everything from the curtains to the bed coverings, which most likely had been red at some point, was now a faded maroon. The single central ceiling light fixture was dust covered and hardly illuminated the room. Fortunately, the bathroom had a shower and appeared clean.

"Let's shower and have an early dinner," Paul suggested. "We can use the hotel dining room. It will be nice to sit at a table for a change."

All we could think about when we returned from a tasty dinner, including a first-time trial of frogs' legs, was a good night's sleep. We would have to be up at 4:00 a.m. to catch the bus back to the police station to register our departure from Canton. Paul pulled back the covers on the bed and I heard him say "scheisse"[63] under his breath. I immediately saw the reason for his dismay. There on the sheets, moving lethargically, were reddish brown ovals. Living in China was a study in entomology. These were bedbugs and any hope of a good night's sleep was now a memory. While I prepared for bed, Paul took a towel and vigorously brushed the surface of the bed, doing his best to reduce the number of bugs that we would come in contact with overnight.

"Our choices are getting bitten or sleeping standing up," Paul

---

63   German word for *shit*.

said. We chose to lie down, swatting away through the night. By morning, we each had several lines of itchy red bites on the exposed skin that had not been covered by our pajamas. It was a relatively small inconvenience that would add color to our tale when we would recount our exodus from China in the days and years to come.

Chapter Forty-Three
Hong Kong Bound
February 28, 1952

Another damp warm morning awaited us as we hurried to close our suitcases. Paul went downstairs to retrieve a bellman to help with the luggage. My hands and feet were so swollen, I could hardly get my stockings and shoes on. I gingerly went down the stairs, tightly gripping the handrail, unable to see the next stair over my bulging belly.

Two armed soldiers stood blocking the entrance to the hotel. We were not allowed to board the bus until, once again, we opened our suitcases, and the soldiers, once again rifled through our belongings. What did they think they would find this time, especially since we were unable to leave the hotel? And how strangely ironic that there was a piece of jewelry worth thousands of dollars in my luggage and they kept missing it.

We boarded the bus with approximately a dozen other foreigners for the ride back to the police station. Our task at the police station now was to register our departure. The clerk at the desk asked for our identification and transit documents. He compared the information with what was recorded the night before, made a notation in his ledger and we reboarded a bus. Upon arrival at the train station, of course, the luggage was inspected again. To this day, the three hour train trip to Hong Kong remains a complete blur. The train was hot and crowded and we were exhausted, itchy and sweaty.

When we arrived in Hong Kong at 4:00 p.m., we were the last to disembark the train. Once we were allowed off the train, we stood next to our suitcases in a long line waiting to be inspected. As foreigners, everyone went before us, including the pigs and chickens that had been brought from farms on the Mainland to be sold in the markets of Hong Kong. When it was our turn, the soldier shouted out an order in Chinese. When we did not respond immediately, he picked up our largest suitcase, released the latches and shook it vigorously, its entire contents lying in the dirt once again. His two underlings took our smaller pieces of luggage and mimicked the actions of their superior. This time, lying there open to everyone to see, lay the diamond brooch. The border guard paid no attention to what lay there in plain sight. He again shouted something in Chinese and signaled us to repack our suitcases, which we did as quickly as possible. I cannot explain why this very valuable piece of jewelry was not confiscated. It seemed like the guards were more interested in humiliating us than in the actual contents of our luggage. This time Paul did not even try to recruit a porter to help with the luggage. He awkwardly juggled our three heavy suitcases and his briefcase. He handed me my vanity to carry, and we walked over the bridge into Hong Kong, the bridge to freedom.

The accountant for US Lines who had worked with Paul in Shanghai was waiting for us at the checkpoint at the other end of the bridge. He stood next to a large, black luxurious looking car. "You can relax now. You are safe," were the first words out of Jack Miller's mouth. The chauffeur ran around the car to retrieve

SHALAMA

our luggage and hoisted it into the trunk of the vehicle. We slid onto the posh leather bench seat in the back and I threw my head back against the headrest, releasing a great sigh of relief as the car pulled away from the turmoil of the checkpoint at the terminus of the bridge. At that moment I closed my eyes as I held Paul's hand resting on the seat next to me. I blocked out the sights and sounds that made up the commotion of Hong Kong. There would be time for sightseeing in the coming week as we prepared for the next part of our journey, the journey that would take us to Europe. I barely heard the conversation Paul was having with the accountant and his response to questions about the desperate situation in Shanghai.

Within a few minutes, the car pulled up in front of what appeared to be a rather posh hotel. As the chauffeur removed the suitcases from the car, a bellman in a red jacket adorned with silver buttons appeared to take our luggage up the carpeted stairs to the lobby. Jack accompanied Paul to the registration desk. I heard him tell the desk clerk, "Mr. and Mrs. Hoffmann will be here until the morning of March 7. All charges related to their stay should be forwarded to the offices of US LInes at 314 Queen's Building." He then told Paul, "The car is at your disposal. Just call the office and we will send it right over. Mr. Carl is looking forward to having dinner with you and Mrs. Hoffmann tomorrow evening." Paul thanked him and we followed the bellman to the elevator that took us to the fifth floor. When the bellman opened the door to our room, a blast of cold air greeted us. Air Conditioning! The hum of a motor confirmed that we were not dreaming! As soon as the bellman shut the door behind him, I was in the white marble bathroom, running warm water to fill the claw foot tub. I sat on the toilet to remove my shoes and stockings. Within moments, all my clothing lay in a heap on the bathroom floor. I called Paul into the bathroom and he helped me step up over the edge of the tub and watched as I lowered myself into warm soothing water.

"Oh, my gosh, Shirley!" Paul exclaimed. For the first time he noticed the swelling of my hands and feet. The seven carat diamond ring made my finger look like a sausage in fancy packaging. "Take some soap and see if you can get that thing off your finger." Paul watched as I lathered up my hands. Try as I might, the ring would not budge. "I'm calling the desk to see if there is a house doctor for the hotel. I'm afraid you are going to lose circulation in that finger." By the time I was out of the bath and dressed in clean clothes, there was a knock on the door. A Chinese man holding a medical bag entered the room and introduced himself as Dr. Ma in perfect British English.

"What seems to be the problem?" he asked.

I held up my right hand. "I can't get it off, I told him.

"That is a problem," he said. "Your fingers are very swollen." Dr. Ma picked up the telephone and after a somewhat lengthy explanation in Chinese, he returned the phone to its cradle. "Someone will be here to help in just a few minutes."

Upon hearing a knock, Paul opened the door to what appeared to be a maintenance man with a basket of tools. Dr. Ma took my hand and held it out for the maintenance man to see while providing instructions in Chinese. The maintenance man rummaged through his tool basket and produced a wire cutter. With Dr. Ma holding my hand steady, palm facing up, the maintenance man nudged a pair of wire cutters under the band of the ring and with a single snap cut through the shiny platinum band. Normal coloring returned to my finger as I pulled the ring off. We thanked the doctor and the maintenance man, repeating again and again how grateful we were for their help, as Paul escorted them to the door.

"Where's that phone number Mary gave you?" Paul asked.

I am calling her contact here and he can come and pick up the ring and the brooch. They can be his problem from now on. We have had one too many close calls because of these two pieces of jewelry."

After dinner in the hotel that night, we retired to our cool comfortable room. There was a radio on the nightstand. Paul turned on the radio and for the first time in three years we heard real news, not the propaganda that the communists were blaring over every frequency in China. I don't know how long Paul listened but I was asleep before I heard the end of the first sentence. For the first time in months I slept soundly. There were no police sirens blaring through the night like in the streets of Shanghai. There were no bedbugs. The phone did not ring. It was wonderfully cool in the room. We pulled up the covers and snuggled closely. We were safe.

Chapter Forty-Four
A Week
Hong Kong February 29 - March 7, 1952

A sliver of bright light streaming in through a space between the curtains woke me as I rolled over in bed the next morning. When I realized Paul was not there, I listened for sounds from the bathroom, but the room was silent. I struggled to right myself among the quilts and the pillows. In the past week I had come to acknowledge how big I was. This baby couldn't come soon enough, but not yet. We still needed to find a place where we could stay for a month or two, where there would be good medical care. As I waddled to the bathroom, I saw a folded piece of paper tented on the table.

It read, "Darling, you looked so peaceful. I did not want to disturb you. I am at the US Lines offices. At 10:00 a.m. I have an appointment with the US Consul General. When you are ready to go out, call the US Lines office and they will send the car.

All my love,
Paul"

I reached for my watch on the nightstand next to bed. It was 9:45 a.m. Paul would be on his way to the Consulate right now.

I dressed and carefully styled my hair and applied my make-up for the first time since we departed Shanghai. Sleeping in the air conditioned room had helped reduce the swelling and I was able to bend my fingers and put on my shoes with greater ease than the day before. When I opened the curtains, clouds were hanging low over Victoria Peak and the harbor. In the distance I could see the funicular that climbed up the mountain. I had heard that Hong Kong was beautiful and from this perspective, it really was quite spectacular.

I took the elevator down to the lobby and found the elegant hotel dining room. The maitre d' guided me to a small round table near a window. I ordered some eggs and toast and a cup of tea. As I ate, I was torn between watching the busy Hong Kong Street scenes and my fellow diners. The relaxed international feel that was Shanghai before the communist takeover still existed here in Hong Kong. People rushed to and fro freely with goal-oriented intention, conducting business, speaking openly to others. In Shanghai, people walked quickly in silence, eyes darting in every direction, with one goal: to arrive at their place of business or home safely without getting interrogated or caught up in a protest. Here in the dining room of the Sunning House, people of every nationality conversed and laughed in careless comfort.

After breakfast, I approached the concierge desk and asked the young woman at the desk to call for the car. I also asked her where would be the best place to purchase baby clothes.

"You have a number of choices Mrs. Hoffmann. There is Shui Hing, Whiteways, and Wing On, all big department stores. It looks like your baby is coming very soon," the concierge commented. "You will find plenty of lovely baby accessories at those stores. You may also find many beautiful handmade items at the smaller shops around town. Your driver will be able to guide you anywhere you may want to go."

"Thank you so much. The baby is due mid-May. Hopefully, it won't arrive too soon. We have a month long journey to Europe to accomplish first. We were limited to what we could carry when we left Shanghai. I think I'll start at Wing On. I did all my shopping in the Shanghai store. I know they have everything. But, first, I need to buy a suitcase. We brought nothing for the baby. We need diapers, bibs, blankets, and outfits. "

"I see the car has arrived," the concierge said. "Have a wonderful day and good luck with the shopping."

"I will," I replied "And could you get a message to my husband that I am out shopping and will meet him here at 5:00 p.m. this evening?"

"Of course, Mrs. Hoffmann."

Hong Kong reminded me of Shanghai; even more crowded, but also more scenic with its surrounding water and hills. Single and double-decker buses, colorfully covered with both Chinese and English advertising, maneuvered their way around raised pagoda-shaped booths from which police officers directed traffic. Fashionably dressed individuals crowded the sidewalks, entering and exiting homes and businesses. Many of the buildings reflected the stylish architecture of British colonialism that had existed in Hong Kong since the Opium Wars in the 1840s.

The day flew by. By 4:30 p.m. I had returned to the hotel to await Paul's arrival. The suitcase I had purchased was three-quarters full with the diapers, bibs, blankets, and baby clothing up to size six months.

I was sitting in an overstuffed armchair with my once again swollen feet propped on an ottoman when my ebullient husband entered the room.

"I don't know where to begin!" he burst out. "It has been an incredible day!" "Except for the two hours I spent at the US Consulate, I have been working the entire day and will have to continue this work through next week as well. I have been writing letters and sending cables, still trying to finalize agreements for clients. I have been requesting and wiring the transfer of funds. Thank goodness this is much easier to accomplish here than in Shanghai."

"What happened at the Consulate," I inquired. This is what I was really interested in hearing.

"When I first arrived there, I was taken into the office of the Political Officer. He had a long list of specific questions and took extensive notes as I related the horrific events we witnessed in Shanghai. I believe his lack of emotion signaled that this was not the first report on the terror the communists had imposed upon the residents of China. He thanked me for the information and escorted me to the office of another official who was responsible for visas. I informed the official that I had requested that our visa files be sent to Milan on February 25, 1952. He told me that he was aware of our case. Apparently the screening process has started. He showed me a letter he had received from Judge Allman requesting that our case be expedited."

"Well that *is* good news! Fingers crossed that there are no more delays. And look what I accomplished today," I sang out. I opened the suitcase filled with baby paraphernalia for Paul to see.

"I see you did what was most important!" he said with a grin. "Put on your prettiest dress. Harold Carl, the manager of US Lines here in Hong Kong, is taking us to the Parisian Grill tonight for dinner. European style food and a piano player. Sounds delightful, doesn't it? The car is picking us up at 7:00 p.m."

This is how it went for the next week. So much to do. So little time! Every night there was dinner with someone else. The Chinese fellow to whom we delivered the brooch and ring took us to lunch at the Repulse Bay Hotel, an incredibly beautiful spot on the island. In between Paul's visits to the US Lines office we squeezed in some sightseeing. Our visit to the race track was cut short by the heat and the crowds. In addition, we had received our cholera vaccinations that morning, which added to our fatigue, so we only stayed long enough to lose eighty cents. Paul made sure to buy a camera in Hong Kong so he could document and send photographs to our families of all our adventures as we traveled. Of course, I wasn't done shopping; there were so many lovely things available at very reasonable prices, especially tablecloths. I do have a passion for beautiful tablecloths! After all, the new suitcase was only three quarters full. Space in a suitcase should never go to waste!

Chapter Forty-Five
Aboard the Felix Roussel
March 7-April 7, 1952

The Felix Roussel would not depart port until 9:00 p.m. on the evening of March 7, 1952. Last-minute tasks included another trip to the US Lines office for Paul. He sent cables to Judge Allman on what he had accomplished during the week and to his parents and sister to let them know that all was well and we would be on our way to Europe that evening. On our way! How wonderful those three words sounded! Although there were violent protests on the Mainland in Kowloon while we were in Hong Kong, we were fortunate not to witness the communist rioters attacking British police officers.

"We cannot get far away from the communists fast enough," Paul remarked. "No one is safe from their unpredictable outbursts."

At 7:00 p.m. the car pulled up in front of Sunning House. Jack Miller, the accountant from US Lines, was there once again to accompany us to the wharf in Victoria Harbor for the next leg of our journey.

"Bon voyage and good luck with the baby. Paul, I hope to see you Stateside soon so we can continue doing business together."

"I hope so, Jack. Thank you for all your help and hospitality while we have been here in Hong Kong. It has been the best week in two years."

We climbed the gang plank and were shown by the bursar to our first-class suite. The ship was just lovely! It was launched in 1929 and was intended for trips between Marseille and Indo-China. During World War II the ship was requisitioned to serve as a troop and evacuation transport manned by British and French volunteers. Now completely refitted with a rich interior, it reflected both European and Indo-Chinese decor. Cast iron panels that lined the corridor walls were a combination of intricate lace work of flowers, vines and animals. Paintings along the hallways included exotic East Indian women, tropical plants and monkeys. On either side of the main staircase leading to the staterooms on the upper deck stood two life size black and gold carved wooden Indian guards. Each day as we passed them we paid our respects.

Within twenty-four hours we had reached Manila. Once again a car was waiting for us. The driver told us he had been instructed to escort us for the next two days, but our first stop would be lunch with Admiral Giles Stedman, former executive officer of the *USS West Point* during World War II, and now the US Lines regional vice president. On the way to the restaurant we saw the total destruction wreaked by the Japanese bombing of Old Manila; not a single building had been left standing. When I entered the restaurant, Mrs. Stedman addressed me. "My dear, you must be so warm with your hat and gloves. They aren't really necessary in Manila." Before leaving Shanghai, all the 'proper' ladies had lectured me on appropriate dress. I had purchased several straw hats and matching pairs of gloves. I was more than relieved to be spared the additional attire in the heat and humidity.

SHALAMA

After Manila, the next port of call was Singapore. Paul had some business to conduct but we were able to squeeze in some sightseeing before we were off to Saigon.

What a blissful trip this was. Between eating and sleeping there was bridge and canasta, and then more eating. We were finally getting some much-needed rest. One thing that never stopped was the letter writing. We were receiving letters from family throughout the trip and Paul was as diligent as ever, writing postcards and letters, keeping everyone informed of our progress and the status of our visas. He really thought we would be in the States by August. Afterall, prominent American businessmen were providing affidavits testifying to the fact that he had saved American lives and protected American funds by remaining in Shanghai.

Saigon would be a three-day adventure in and of itself. The fight between the French colonialists and the communists had already begun. More than once we were ordered below deck due to sniper fire while sailing up the Mekong River to reach the port. Once we disembarked, we could not believe the heat. It was unbearable. One would think we would be used to this having lived in Shanghai all these years, but the heat here took it to a whole other level. You could feel the scorching pavement radiating up through your shoes. We didn't see very much having to stop frequently to sit and have a drink. My feet and legs swelled so badly that our last stop before reboarding was to a shoe store for a new pair of shoes. We did not disembark again. During the next two days French women and their children who were being evacuated joined us on board. I sat on deck running my hand over my ever growing belly, imagining myself in their position. It was difficult enough making this long trip knowing my unborn child, at least for the time being, was safe inside me. Here were these women with young children, toddlers and infants, most unaccompanied by male relatives; husbands, fathers and brothers stayed behind to fight the communist foes, to protect homes and businesses. The goal of these women was the same as every mother, to protect their children. My baby did not yet have a face or a name, but I saw his or her face in every child that came aboard. I, and every other mother aboard the Felix Roussel knew we were among the lucky ones. The morning after our departure we read in the ship's paper that a bomb intended for our ship exploded on the pier one hour after we set sail.

On board the Felix Roussel we became acquainted with a Chinese woman who was traveling with her five year old daughter. Her name was Agnes DaCosta and she had married a Portuguese colonel who was stationed in Macau. Agnes was originally from Hong Kong and Sandra had been born in Macau. They were now traveling to Lisbon to rejoin the Colonel. Paul played with Sandra endlessly, spinning his wedding band on the table and magically pulling coins out of her ears. He taught her all the suits in a deck of cards, inventing matching and memory games as he went along, while Agnes and I observed, sipping cool drinks on the deck.

"He is going to be a wonderful father," Agnes commented when Sandra giggled as Paul twirled her around the deck in a spontaneous dance.

"I have no doubt about that," I responded. "We just need to get somewhere in time to have this baby safely. As badly as I want to be relieved of all this weight and swelling, I just hope we find a cooler, cleaner, safer place for the delivery. We have been in limbo for so long I don't even let myself imagine where we will be when it finally comes time to deliver. All I know is that we are heading for Europe and the baby may be the one to decide what happens next."

SHALAMA

The next week became a jumble of memories, intermingled with some unforgettable moments. It was refreshing to be able to have dinner off the ship at our next stop, Colombo, the capital city of Ceylon. As opposed to Manila with all its destruction and Saigon with its heat and unrest, Colombo was relatively calm and welcoming for our brief sojourn. It had been a British colony until just four years earlier, and like Hong Kong reflected the British presence. Always one to want to experiment with the local cuisine, I ordered a curry dish from the menu at the lovely harborside restaurant that was recommended by one of the crew as we left the ship earlier in the day. While I was enjoying my dinner of chicken, vegetables and rice, Paul helped himself to a generous forkful from my plate. He immediately grabbed his beer to wash down what he had just placed in his mouth. From the expression on his face, for a moment I thought he might spit it out onto the ground. "How can you eat that?" he exclaimed. "I never tasted anything that hot!"

"I'm not sure I disagree with you, but it tastes good to me," I replied with a chuckle.

After dinner we strolled leisurely back to the ship. The setting sun provided a little bit of relief from the heat that was a constant on this island off the southern coast of India. Every few feet we were accosted by peddlers offering to sell us rubies. "Madam! Madam, Sir!" the peddlers shouted. "So cheap! You want buy ruby?" They directed their sales pitch to Paul, "Lady really like ruby."

"I would love to buy you one of these beautiful stones," said Paul. "But how do we know if they are really rubies? They could be garnets, or even glass and be worth practically nothing."

"It would be perfectly frivolous to buy any jewelry right now. We have no idea what we will need our money for in the coming months," I replied.

"Very true. As always my practical wife. I can always depend on your common sense," said Paul as he took my hand into the crook of his elbow and led me up the gang plank of the Felix Roussel.

The next day, on the way from Colombo to Djibouti, Paul had spent a little too much time on deck in the midday sun as we sailed from the Indian Ocean into the Arabian Sea. When he returned to our cabin his clothes were drenched in sweat and he complained of a headache and dizziness. I summoned the ship's doctor.

"A mild case of heatstroke," the doctor said. "Plenty of liquids, bed rest and keep out of the sun. There is no escaping the intensity of the heat and humidity in this part of the world." I expressed my relief that it was nothing more serious and thanked the doctor.

"I'm a little disappointed," the doctor commented as he turned to place his stethoscope into his medical bag, which was open on the chair beside the bed. "I thought for certain you were calling me to welcome your little one into the world. Better luck next time, I suppose."

"It's still a little too soon for this baby to make its debut. Sorry to disappoint," I responded.

"Only joking, of course," said the doctor. "Better to deliver on terra firma, for sure," he said as he bid us good night.

We would have one more stop on the Horn of Africa, the tiny country of Djibouti, before entering the Red Sea on our way to Egypt. Once again it was brutally hot and we would only be in port for a few hours. Before disembarking we were warned that the pick pockets of Djibouti were exceptionally bold. This did not come as a surprise when we were overwhelmed by scenes of abject poverty and beggars that lined the streets, many with open sores. "Watch my pockets," Paul called out to me as he aimed his camera to document our ship in port. No sooner had he said this, than a young boy, no more than ten or twelve years of age, whipped Paul's gold wire rimmed eyeglasses right off his nose. Paul stepped back in disbelief, almost dropping the camera.

"Can't say we weren't warned," he said. "Fortunately, I have another pair in our luggage." When we returned to the ship at least three other passengers reported they too had been relieved of their eyeglasses in Djibouti. "I suppose we are lucky, that is all that was lost today," Paul said.

From Djibouti, we would continue on to Suez. At dinner the next night, the ship's bursar announced, "For all those interested, the Thomas Cook Travel Agency is offering a land tour from Suez to Cairo to Port Said, while the ship passes through the Suez Canal. Any passengers that elect to take the tour will rejoin us in Port Said." I felt a tap on my shoulder. It was the ship's doctor who was sitting at the table next to us.

"You aren't considering taking this tour, are you?" he asked. "It is going to be a very long and hot day. Besides how uncomfortable you will be in the heat, you don't want to trigger an early labor here. I think this is the last place on earth you would want to have this baby, if the baby chooses this to be the time to make its grand entrance." I had come to trust this doctor. He clearly had my best interest, and the interest of my baby at heart.

"As tempting as it is to see the wonders of ancient Egypt, I think I will let Paul go on this one alone."

The next morning Paul joined the other passengers that had signed up for the tour on the foredeck. "Are you sure it's alright for me to go?" Paul asked.

"Of course," I said. "Why shouldn't you go? We have no idea when we will be back in this part of the world. Don't miss the opportunity."

"Do you know how much I love you, Darling? You are the most selfless person on the planet, and the most reasonable. Thank you so much for allowing me this chance. You know I would rather have you with me to experience this together, but Lord knows this quick trip will be way too strenuous for you and the baby. I promise to take lots of photos and tell you everything when I get back this evening."

We embraced and I watched Paul and about twenty or so other passengers descend the gang plank to the jeeps bearing the Thomas Cook logo that were waiting to take them on their excursion.

I found a chaise lounge under an overhang near our cabin to avoid the sun and asked the cabin boy to bring me a cup of tea. I spent a good portion of the day on that chaise with my feet up reading a current *Life* magazine, as opposed to the ones that were months old that circulated the offices of the Gas Company in Shanghai. I dozed off repeatedly as the ship slowly moved north through the Suez Canal from Suez to Port Said. I did not give too much thought to where Paul was and what he might be doing until after dinner when it occurred to me that the group had not yet returned and the ship was scheduled to depart Port Said in the next few hours. I positioned myself at the rail on the deck so I could watch for the returning passengers. There was no shortage of activity to watch in this busy port. The Felix Roussel was dwarfed by the shadows of the smokestacks of huge ocean liners and cargo ships on either side of the wharf. Smaller boats jockeyed for position as nets full of fish were being brought ashore. In the distance the minaret of a mosque stood out above the skyline. The streets were as crowded as any port we had visited with a collection of pedestrians in an assortment of Western and Middle-Eastern dress; from pith-helmeted British soldiers all dressed in white to 'faceless' Muslim women completely concealed in black burkas walking behind fez-wearing men in white kaftans and western-style suit jackets.

It was after dark when I finally saw Paul approaching our boat, waving his straw hat in the air to get my attention. By the time he reached where I was standing on deck, he was breathless from running. He gave me a brief hug; he was sweaty, gritty with fine sand on his face and clothing, and somewhat smelly. "That's the essence of camel you're smelling," Paul said. "As promised, I have so much to tell you!" Paul exclaimed. "First a shower and a change of clothing!" I had to agree that was the priority. I finally let out a long slow breath admitting to myself that I had begun to worry. The group had been scheduled to return two hours earlier.

We spent what was left of the evening on deck chairs enjoying a bit of respite from the heat. Cooling sea breezes began to fill the evening air as the Felix Roussel navigated its way into the Mediterranean Sea.

"Every time I think I have had the most unusual experience yet, I have one more. I can add today to my ever growing list," Paul began. ""I really thought that the pyramids and the sphinx were going to be the highlights, but we arrived there in the heat of the day. Walking around these stone wonders to appreciate their scale was out of the question. We did take a short camel ride which helped the imagination envision life in ancient Egypt. It never ceases to amaze how the ingenuity of humans can create amazing structures where there is nothing. After the pyramids in the desert, the mosque we visited in the city was awe-inducing. The structure was itremendous, with ceilings maybe thirty or forty feet high. Hundreds of symmetrically lined columns defined the space. The temperature must have dropped twenty degrees when we stepped onto the cool stone floors. As we exited the mosque we got a first-hand look at the congestion that is Cairo. Trolleys whizzed by with as many people hanging on the outside of the trolleys, clinging to each other like clusters of beetles, as were jammed on the inside. It's a wonder no one fell off as the trolley accelerated around the corners. The museum in Cairo was incredible. There were so many of the treasures of the pharaohs, including the artifacts from the tomb of Tutankhamen. I can't wait to develop the film in the camera so you can see all of this."

By this time my eyelids had begun to flutter. It had been an incredibly long day.

"Were you trying to see everything in the museum? Was that what delayed your arrival this evening?" This was my last question before I would be heading off to bed.

"No. That would have been too simple," Paul said. "Things have been very tense in Cairo since an anti-British uprising about a month ago. We were stopped at a British military checkpoint for close to an hour. The Thomas Cook people had failed to inform the checkpoint about our group and there were several angry phone calls before we were allowed to continue on. For a while there, we were concerned that we would not arrive in Port Said in time to meet up with the Felix Roussel."

"I'm beyond glad you made it. Standing at the railing on deck waiting for you, I had this momentary vision of the boat pulling away without you. After all we've been through, to get to this point...My voice trailed off. My energy for the day was spent. Paul helped me to my feet. "I'm off to bed now. See you in the morning, Love."

I left Paul sitting on the deck, cigarette in his right hand, gin and tonic in his left, staring at the reflection of the moon on the quiet waters of the Mediterranean.

Chapter Forty-Six
Marseille in View
First Week of April 1952

I awoke the next morning, to an empty bed beside me. I thought for sure that Paul would still be sound asleep after the events of the day before. Not knowing where to begin to look for him, I opened the cabin door and there he stood leaning over the railing.

"Good morning, Darling. I couldn't sleep. Thirteen years is a long time. I often wondered what returning to Europe would feel like. What changes did the War bring? Look, the port of Marseille lies ahead. For the first time in thirteen years, and in your lifetime, we will blend in with the crowd. How strange that will be."

"I never gave that any thought. I've never been anywhere where most everyone wasn't Chinese. Yet, somehow, we managed to stay separate in our own small community. Why was that? I think it was because we were so very different. But, the beauty of it was we respected each other's differences. No one was out to change anyone. No one claimed that one culture was superior to the other. So we were able to live side by side."

"I think you are right," said Paul. "It was the Nazi and Japanese claims of ethnic superiority that caused the awful, horrific events that the entire world has suffered. I suppose we were among the lucky who benefited from living within Chinese society. It is so unfortunate the communist takeover has put an end to coexistence as we knew it. It was by no means perfect, and there clearly were injustices, but it felt civilized. A civilized society can move forward and get better. Maybe that is what we can hope for in America."

I watched Paul stare out across the Mediterranean Sea. His serene countenance was reflected in the calm waters that still stretched for miles. We would not be arriving in Marseille until late afternoon.

"At this moment," said Paul, "Everything is so quiet, so peaceful. Have I had a day that compares in the last thirteen years? I don't think so."

I put my arm around Paul's waist and he put his around mine; a big stretch given the size of my belly. For several minutes we pulled each other close and savored the tranquility. We both knew that by the end of the day the hustle and bustle that we knew, our normal existence, would return.

"I really could stand here all day," I said. "But this baby says it's time for some breakfast and we have some packing to do."

Paul kissed me on the cheek. "Let's go feed the baby. I like how that sounds."

As we approached the port of Marseille, my mind drifted back to December of 1940, standing at the rail with Papa as the ship slowly maneuvered up the Whangpoo River. I remembered the excitement and curiosity as I clutched Papa's hand, pummeling him with questions. Soon I would be the parent. My baby would have no memory of this journey. If my child was standing beside me asking questions, I would have no answers. Did Papa really know what lay ahead of us?

As the Felix Roussel approached the harbor, it was less than apparent how a boat of significant size could possibly navigate the congregation of vessels that appeared to populate every possible space along the wharves and piers. The buildings of Marseille were separated from dockside by a single roadway and the commotion of the harbor was reminiscent of both Shanghai and Hong Kong. I felt a hand touch my forearm and Agnes was standing beside me with little Sandra clutching her hand.

"Do you know where you'll be spending the night, Shirley?" Agnes asked. "We are headed for Lisbon by train tomorrow morning. It is too late in the day to try and leave now."

"We will be heading to the American Consulate in Milan tomorrow to check on our visas, also by train. We won't try to leave tonight either. I think Paul has gone to inquire about a hotel for tonight," I replied.

"Might we accompany you and Paul. I'd be more comfortable knowing you were both nearby. Maybe we could find a place to have dinner together after we get settled."

"I'm sure Paul will be fine with that." Just then Paul approached from the other direction on the deck.

"I spoke with the bursar and he recommended that we stay at the Château d'Harve. It is practically dockside, not too expensive and it will be easy to get to the train station in the morning."

"Agnes would like to join us," I said.

"Of course! I would love to spend more time with my favorite girl," he said, giving Sandra a wink.

We each took a piece of hand luggage. Paul arranged for both our luggage and Agnes' to be brought directly to the hotel. We descended the gangplank to the sidewalk and leisurely strolled towards the hotel. For once we were not assaulted by the heat. We found our hotel easily and crossed the road to the entrance.

We quickly saw why the hotel was inexpensive. There was no elevator but fortunately our rooms were only on the second floor. We were given large heavy metal keys. Paul put the key in the key hole of the wooden door and flung it open.

"Well that's unusual," said Paul. I peaked over his shoulder to see a large claw foot bathtub in the middle of the room.

"Not much privacy if you want to take a bath," I said laughing. "You can be sure that won't stop me!"

We arranged to meet Agnes and Sandra in the lobby in an hour to go to dinner. We found Agnes speaking to the concierge. When she turned and saw us, she said, "I was inquiring about the best place for bouillabaisse."

"Bouillabaisse? What's that?" I asked.

"It's this marvelous fish stew that the French make," said Agnes. There is no better place to try it than right here in Marseille where it originated, by the harbor where all the fish are brought in daily."

The weather was mild enough for alfresco dining. We proceeded to the bistro that the concierge had recommended. Soup bowls with seafood broth and grilled slices of bread covered with a rouille[64] were brought to the table first. No sooner had we finished our broth than the waiter placed a large platter of three different fish and an assortment of vegetables that included leeks, tomatoes, onion and celery in the center of the table. The aroma was heavenly and we ate heartily. As the sun set over the harbor we sipped our wine while sopping up what was left of the vibrantly spiced and herbed broth with the crusty French bread that the waiter had kindly replenished several times.

"Tomorrow will be the first day of the rest of our lives," Paul commented.

---

64 Sauce of egg yolk, olive oil, bread crumbs, garlic, saffron and cayenne pepper served as a garnish with fish soups and stews.

SHALAMA

"For us too," said Agnes. "Sandra hasn't seen her Daddy for almost a year. She will be starting school in the fall. And I will be the Chinese wife of a Portuguese colonel living in Lisbon. It will be very different from when we were stationed in Macau."

"Our lives, yours and ours, have been defined by change. As hard as it was to leave Vienna when I was just eighteen years old under such difficult conditions, leaving my parents and all that was familiar behind, I feel extremely fortunate. Not only did we survive the War when so many lost everything, Shanghai was an irreplaceable education. I went from the insularity of Vienna where everyone spoke one language, ate one type of food, and everyone dressed the same, to the multicultural cornucopia that was Shanghai. I think we are well prepared for whatever comes next," said Paul.

After dinner we took a leisurely stroll with Agnes and Sandra along the waterfront. Sandra ran right up to the water's edge, eager to throw pebbles in the water, mesmerized by the splash and their disappearance below the surface. Paul entertained her by skipping stones across the water, encouraging Sandra to count the number of skips. She gleefully applauded his effort as he tried to increase the number of skips from the previous throw. When we arrived at the hotel lobby the four of us exchanged hugs and wishes of *bonne chance* and *bon voyage*, accompanied by promises to keep in touch. Our train would be leaving at 6:25 a.m. and there would be no opportunity for goodbyes in the morning.

"Isn't it amazing that after just thirty days together we became so close," Agnes said."I will miss you terribly. Here is our mailing address in Lisbon. Be sure to send pictures of the baby!"

"And we will miss you, too! I won't forget all your valuable advice. We can only hope our baby will be as delightful as your beautiful Sandra," I said as we embraced for a final time before saying good night.

Chapter Forty-Seven
Where to Next?
Second Week of April 1952

The calling out of the boatmen and fisherman bringing in the daily catch awakened us at the break of day. We welcomed the cacophony of the port since we knew we needed to be up early to catch the train to Milan. Our plan was to go straight to the American Consulate to check on the status of our visas to the United States. We had laid out our clothes the night before and were all dressed and packed within a half hour. Paul called for the bellman to help us down to the lobby with the luggage. We ducked quickly into the hotel restaurant and downed a coffee and croissant while the concierge hailed a cab for us. The ride to the train station was short and before we knew it we were comfortably situated in a first class car for our six and a half-hour train ride to Milan. The views of the Mediterranean from the window were breathtaking as the train meandered north along the French Riviera. Not until Genoa did we lose the views of coastline and water when the train turned inward towards Milan.

All the way to Milan, Paul could not stop talking about the

architecture of Milan, the Duomo and how he had read about it and seen pictures of it as a child. As our train pulled into the station shortly before 2:00 p.m. we were immediately impressed by the massive train station with its high curved ceiling and marble floors. There was little time to admire its beauty since our goal was to arrive at the American Consulate before it closed for the evening. It was the week of Good Friday and Easter and we knew that everything would be shutting down for the long Easter weekend. If there were any papers to process, we wanted to get a jump on it. In true lawyerly fashion, Paul came prepared with documentation that he had first applied for a visa to the United States on March 4, 1947 under the Austrian quota. He had been interviewed at the American Consulate in December of 1948 and was informed that no quota number was available. On January 30,1950 we received word from the American Consulate General that my registration for a visa under the Austrian quota had been confirmed. Early in the fall of 1950 the American Consulate closed and we were informed that our file was forwarded to the American Embassy, Consular Section in Italy on October 6, 1950. On February 25, 1952, three days before leaving Shanghai, Paul informed the Embassy that we would be in Italy by early April. During his visit to the American Consulate General in Hong Kong on March 5, 1952, Paul had completed the necessary political screening forms. It was his understanding that our papers would be forwarded to Milan.

We quickly found a porter to help take the luggage off the train and find a taxi. Thankfully, the taxi driver readily understood our very poor Italian when we directed him to take us to the American Consulate on Via Principe Amadeo. The driver generously carried our luggage up the steps of the Consulate. Paul thanked him effusively and pressed some extra lira into his hand. There were two overstuffed couches in the foyer of the

Consulate and I gratefully lowered myself into the one nearest the entrance.

"Wait here while I find out what happens next," Paul instructed. "I'll come and get you if they want to talk with you, too."

It must have been forty-five minutes to an hour later when Paul reappeared. I am sure I dozed off while he was gone. I could tell by the look on his face when he returned that the news was not all good.

"There is no visa section in Milan," he said. "When I informed the Embassy we were leaving Shanghai, our dossier was forwarded to Genoa, where there is a visa section. But, the news is not all bad. Genoa is less than a hundred miles away and we will have the next couple of days to see this beautiful city. With the Easter weekend approaching there is no rush to get to Genoa. We won't be able to get there in time to accomplish anything, so we might as well just enjoy Milan."

Our first task was to find somewhere to stay. We asked for a recommendation from the carabinieri[65] stationed on the sidewalk in front of the Consulate, and he directed us to a small establishment only a few blocks away. The officer took one look at me with my bulging belly, raised his arm in the air and within moments, a cab pulled up to the curb. He graciously helped load our luggage into the cab and directed the driver to take us to Casa Rinaldo, which was less than a five-minute ride away. After what seemed to be a lengthy discussion in broken Italian between Paul and the desk clerk, we had a room for the next two nights.

Once we were situated in our room, Paul said, "We can't be in Milan without attending the opera at La Scala. Italy is the birthplace of opera and La Scala is one of the premier venues in

---

65 Police officer.

the world. You put your feet up and rest. I'm going to see if I can get us tickets for tonight or tomorrow."

Chapter Forty-Eight
Milan
Second Week of April 1952

Within the hour, Paul was back grinning like the Cheshire Cat from Alice in Wonderland.

"Two tickets for tonight's performance of *The Abduction from the Seraglio* by Mozart. First balcony seats. Maria Callas, the coloratura soprano is performing. I hear she is incredible."

"I hope we have time for dinner," I said. "Right now this baby is screaming for something to eat." With all the excitement of the day, we hadn't eaten anything since we grabbed sandwiches from the club car on the train.

"Of course," said Paul. "I got a recommendation from the desk clerk on my way in for a restaurant near La Scala and the performance isn't until 8:00 p.m. That should be enough time to have dinner."

Once again we were in a cab, this time on our way to the restaurant. We ordered a half carafe of house red wine, chicken puttanesca and linguini. To say it was delicious was an understatement! This was the first time I had eaten Italian food and if this was an example of what Italian food was like, I was already looking forward to our next meal. We were so intent on savoring every morsel, I don't think we said two words to each other throughout the entire meal. As soon as we were done, Paul signaled the waiter to bring the check. His eyes practically popped out of his head upon examining the check.

"What's wrong?" I asked.

"I guess meat is still very expensive here in Europe. It looks like post-war shortages still dictate prices. This chicken was worth its weight in gold. We'll have to be more careful in our choices from now on. But, for now let's consider it a treat to celebrate our arrival in Europe and get to the opera."

We paid the check and Paul helped me out of my chair. It was 7:45 p.m. and we only had a two-block walk to Teatro alla Scala. The sun had set and floodlights illuminated the facade of the majestic building. We joined the formally dressed crowd in the lobby. Paul showed our tickets to an usher and he directed us to an elevator towards the back of the theater. "*Pisa Cinque*", he said. We exited the elevator to find, yes, indeed, we were in the first balcony, the only balcony. Paul had failed to realize that the four lower level seats were boxes. In the balcony individual wooden seats were extremely narrow and crammed in one next to the other. Of course, our seats were in the middle of the row. Everyone had to stand as we said "*scuzi*" repeatedly and squeezed by. My embarrassment was mitigated by the smiles of the other opera fans realizing my condition. I pressed my hand into my belly as I passed them, as if I could make it smaller as I inched my way to my seat. The real challenge was lowering myself into the seat. I hardly fit. It was hard to appreciate the stunning red velvet curtains and seats in the gold-painted boxes below from where we sat. As the house lights dimmed and the overture floated up to the balcony, so did the heat of the day. I wish I could say that the great Maria Callas singing a Mozart opera was a highlight of our introduction to Europe. Unfortunately, my discomfort trumped enjoyment of the performance that night.

Somehow we managed to stay for the entire performance. When we stepped back onto the sidewalk on our way back to the hotel, I took a huge deep breath as we were met by the cool evening air.

"I am so sorry, Darling, I had no idea," said Paul. When they offered me first balcony seats, I assumed La Scala's design was similar to the *Wiener Staatsoper* in Vienna. First balcony in Vienna has excellent seats.

"I can't blame you for the small seats. But, I do blame you for this," I exclaimed pointing to my big belly. We both laughed as we made our way back to the hotel.

CHAPTER FORTY-NINE
Genoa to Venice to Vienna
Mid-April - Mid-May 1952

The next day we fulfilled Paul's dream of seeing the Duomo in Milan before catching a train for Genoa, where we would finally be able to check the status of our visas to the United States. The facade of this Gothic cathedral with its multiple spires was truly a sight to behold.

"It is more majestic than I even could've imagined!," exclaimed Paul. "It's simply breathtaking! The *Stephansdom* in Vienna in the *Stephansplatz*, the main square, is nowhere near in size or artistic architecture. You'll be able to see for yourself when we arrive in Vienna. Before we go to Vienna we'll stop in Venice, another example of Italian brilliance and beauty. I was smitten with Venice when I visited in 1938 on my way to Shanghai. We are so close and I don't want you to miss seeing it. Who knows when we will be able to return to Europe once we have arrived in the States."

I could not deny Paul's enthusiasm and desire to share his appreciation of some of the most awe inspiring sights the European continent had to offer. Truth be told, despite the challenges of my advanced pregnancy, I too, felt like a kid in a candy shop, eagerly looking for the next treat that would be offered and unable to say no. So far, France and Italy did not disappoint. I was running out of fingers to count the number of places we had visited since leaving Shanghai two months earlier. I suppose having just turned twenty-four years old I was young and strong enough, not to mention naive, as well, to not think twice about grabbing every opportunity for another adventure.

From the Duomo we hailed a taxi to the train station and caught the noon train to Genoa. The train was incredibly crowded. It was Good Friday and everyone seemed to be heading to the Italian Riviera for the long Easter weekend. As we boarded the train, a gentleman noticed my condition and promptly offered me a seat. Poor Paul spent the next two and a half-hours wedged in on the platform between the train cars. We arrived in Genoa by mid-afternoon and were advised by a carabinieri at the entrance to the station that there was a pensione within a short distance from the train station that would have suitable accommodations. It was also the third day of Passover. It was the very first time in my life that I had not participated in a Seder, which felt very strange. I had mentioned this to Paul, and upon checking in at the pensione he inquired of the clerk where he might obtain some matzah. Fortunately, the clerk was familiar with the nearby Jewish Community Center and gave Paul instructions where to find it. Later that afternoon, Paul said he was going out for a quick walk and returned with a box of matzah. That night at dinner, we heard quiet laughter at the table behind us. It came from another emigrant Jew, apparently having dinner with some friends. When we made eye contact, he pointed to the matzah on my plate and then to the large chunk of Italian bread on

Paul's plate. "*Zissen Pesach! Shabbat Shalom!*"[66] he said. We raised our wine glasses and returned his holiday wishes. I couldn't help thinking about Papa. At least, after reciting "Next year in Jerusalem " at the Seder table for so many years, Papa was able to celebrate one Passover holiday in the Promised Land.

Since Easter Monday is a holiday in Italy, we had three glorious days to relax and explore Genoa. On Saturday we found a bus that would take us to Nervi, the first town on the Italian Riviera. It was gorgeous. There was no end to the magnificent views of the Mediterranean Sea.

"Wouldn't it be nice if we could stay here to await our visas?" Paul commented. "But, I don't think we could afford it. With views like these, this place must be very expensive."

On the morning of Tuesday, April 16, 1952 we were first in line at the Visa Section of the American Consulate. We were escorted into an inner office where a portly gentleman dressed in a gray suit and tie sat behind a large wooden desk. We told him who we were and he asked us to please wait while he went to retrieve our file. He returned just a few minutes later with a rather thick portfolio.

"I see you have been applying for a visa as a displaced person since 1947," the official said to Paul.

"Yes," Paul replied. "It has been a long and chaotic five years since that first application. When I met my wife in 1949, she was stateless. We were married in a Chinese civil ceremony so that I could put her on my Austrian passport before the Austrian Consulate shut down in Shanghai. Then we were not allowed to leave China until all the accounts held by the law firm I represented were settled."

"I see that documentation here as well as affidavits of support

---

66   A sweet Passover and a peaceful Sabbath.

from Erich Hoffmann and Karl Heinz Praeger. What is your connection to these individuals?"

"Erich Hoffmann is my first cousin and Karl Heinz Praeger is my brother-in-law, married to my sister," Paul replied.

"And where do they reside?" the official queried.

"Both live with their families in Boston, Massachusetts."

"It appears that all the necessary paperwork is here," the official said."It will have to be reviewed. You'll have to wait for further notification. I don't expect you will hear anything before July 1," he said.

We thanked the official for his time and exited the building. Glorious morning aromas emanated from a sidewalk cafe on the next block. There was a sunny table with two chairs available so we sat down and ordered coffee and fresh rolls.

As we waited for our breakfast, Paul said, "Well this makes our next steps easier. If nothing is going to happen before July 1, we will have plenty of time to go to Vienna to have the baby and find out the status of the apartments Grandfather Singer left to me and my cousins. But, first it will be Venice, one of the most magnificent places on this earth!"

The next morning, once again we were on a train, this time from Genoa to Venice. As we chugged along the top of the Italian 'boot', I lay my head on Paul's shoulder with his hand held firmly in my lap. The serenity of the landscape was mirrored in our hearts. There were no more watchful eyes and inspections of our luggage. In Venice, there would be no Consulate visits and interviews. For the next few days we would have a true vacation, hopefully enough to prepare us for what would await us when we arrived in Vienna. Both Paul and I dozed off into a comfortable sleep. Before we knew it the six hour train ride had passed and we were in Venezia Santa Lucia Rail Station.

We boarded a vaporetto[67] which took us across the Grand Canal to the docks near the Campanile di San Marco, adjacent to the Dowager's Palace at the entrance to St. Mark's Square. Paul had booked a hotel for us before leaving Genoa.

When we asked a local resident where our hotel was, he took one look at me and said, *"Too far for Mama! Gondola molto bene,"* while pointing to a black and gold boat with a very handsome young Italian with blue eyes and curly brown hair. The gondolier jumped ashore and introduced himself as Enrico. Enrico took our suitcases and lowered them into the center of the gondola. Keeping one foot on the side of the gondola to hold it steady against the shore, Enrico signaled Paul to step down into the boat to get ready to receive me. Enrico held me firmly under the elbow as I gingerly put one foot on the cushioned seat and stepped down onto the bottom of the gondola into Paul's arms. After we had taken our seats, Enrico hopped to the back of the gondola, grabbed his long oar and shoved off from the shore. Within a few minutes, we had taken a turn into one of the smaller canals that serve as the roadways of Venice. As we passed under one of the small bridges that connect the sidewalks on either side of the canals, Enrico's deep baritone voice belted out an Italian love song. Paul turned to him and asked, "Enrico Caruso?" and gave him a thumb's up.

We were blessed with glorious late April weather for the three days we were in Venice. We saw all the sights there were to see; the Bridge of Sighs, the Rialto Bridge, the Dowager's Palace, and the Cathedral. Our leisurely walks ended every day at St. Mark's Square, where I took great pleasure in feeding the pigeons. After the bag of bird food we had bought from one of the many street vendors was gone, it was, of course, time to feed ourselves. A

---

[67] Water bus.

glass of wine and savory fresh fish were accompanied by shifting shadows cast by the surrounding buildings of the piazza as the sun dissolved into darkness.

CHAPTER FIFTY
Reflections on an Interlude
Connecticut 2003

"I remember the picture of you in Venice!" exclaimed Cara. "You're down on one knee in front of the Cathedral feeding the birds! You can't even tell you are pregnant!"

"My coat disguised how far along I was in my pregnancy. We had many letters from Oma and Opa warning Papa to be more careful and considerate of my health and the health of the baby. We wrote back that I was doing well and enjoying every moment of our explorations and adventures! Why not? We could not contain the excitement we felt because we were free to do what we pleased. "And Venice! Such a glorious place! That's why Papa had to take me there and decided to take you and your cousin, Rebecca, there three years ago. He never forgot how we enjoyed it in '52."

"Weren't you concerned about having the baby too soon?" Cara asked.

"It was our first baby. What did we know? The doctor said mid-May. Don't doctors know everything? Very soon we were going to find out they don't!"

Chapter Fifty-One
Return to Vienna
April 19 - May 22, 1952

The morning of April 19, 1952, found us once again on a twelve hour train ride from Venice to Vienna. I had grown to love these long peaceful interludes of calm rocking motion that quieted the active baby inside me, who was clearly running out of room to stretch its growing limbs. But, I sensed that Paul was not experiencing the same delightful mellow mood as when we traveled through France and Italy.

"Is something wrong," I asked? "You seem jittery this morning."

"The borders between Italy and Austria are still controlled by the Russians. Even though I know we are carrying legal documentation, I don't trust the Russian border guards not to question your passport."

"Can we save the worrying until something actually happens?"

"I only wish I had your disposition," Paul replied. "Maybe some of your optimistic thinking will rub off on me as time goes by."

I took his hand and assumed the familiar position of my head on his shoulder and drifted off to sleep for the next hour or so. When I awoke the train had come to a stop and uniformed Russian guards came down the aisle asking for passports. We were at the Austrian border. A tall broad shouldered young man in his mid-twenties took my passport and spent an unusually long time looking at it.

"*Dobre utra*," he said.

I intentionally hesitated, "Oh yes, good morning," I responded.

"You speak Russian?" he asked.

"Just a little. I was born and raised in China. Everyone spoke English in Shanghai," I replied. It was only a partial lie. Yes, I was born in China and English was the lingua Franca in the international community, but I still could converse in Russian with the best of them.

The officer handed me back my passport and I could see the relief flood through Paul's body. For the rest of the trip he was able to enjoy the magnificent views of the springtime glory of the Tyrol in the distance as the train continued on to Vienna.

When the train arrived in Vienna, or *Wien* as it is called in German, we took a cab to the small apartment of a gentile friend of Paul's parents, a Mrs. Wanke, who had remained in Vienna through the War years. When we saw the size of her apartment, we quickly realized that her generous offer to stay with her until the baby was born was unrealistic. Within a week, Paul had found a two-bedroom apartment in one of the outlying districts in the American Zone, as far away from the Soviet Zone as possible. Knowing that the Chinese communists had come to arrest him the day we left Shanghai, he did everything in his power to avoid contact with the Soviet occupation forces and all things communist.

SHALAMA

A few days after we moved into our new flat, Paul wrote excitedly to his parents:

"Our new flat is in the 18th District, twenty minutes from *Schottentor* in *Gersthof, Witthauerstrasze* 17/7. It faces east and we have lovely morning sun. There is plenty of room for our things. A baby bed will be lent to us. There is a garden downstairs, and of course, we have use of the bathroom and kitchen. The landlady is very nice and we have the services of a maid. So there is nothing to complain about. I do the marketing and Shirley does the cooking."

It would have been more accurate to say I was learning to cook Paul's favorite Austrian and Viennese delicacies. He would return from the market with a collection of groceries, some of which he would have to identify as I had never seen some of the ingredients he had chosen for that night's meal. Often, our landlady was standing nearby as the bags were unloaded onto the kitchen table and gave a wry smile as Paul eagerly explained the *knoedel*[68], *goulash* or *schnitzel* that his mother prepared. She would look at me and say "I will help," which was greatly appreciated.

Paul was not so well received on the morning he brought home an entire cow's head from the market, hoping for cow's brains for dinner that night. The maid happened to be walking past the kitchen. Upon seeing the bovine decapitation, she let out a scream and ran out the door. An hour later, her brother was at the door asking what had caused such an upset to his sister. She asked him to retrieve her things saying she "would not enter that house again!" Our landlady explained what had happened and assured the maid's brother that it was safe for her to return if she chose to do so.

---

68   Dumplings.

Paul's letters to his family always contained news of the Austrian football league, with detailed descriptions of games and players for his father's enjoyment, recounts of visits with friends and relatives who were in Vienna and their plans for the future, and reviews of Paul's other love, the opera. Somehow we squeezed in performances of the *Die Fleidermaus, Die Verkaufte Braute*[69], Tosca, and Johnny Belinda, plus a theater performance of Cyrano de Bergerac, all within the two weeks before the pending arrival of the baby.

It was our good fortune that Paul's father's cousin, Dr. Irwin Lengyel, had returned to Vienna after spending the war years in Yu Yao, a port city about 100 miles south of Shanghai, at a missionary hospital serving a population of about 100,000 Chinese. Irwin found an obstetrician, who determined I was in excellent health. Irwin made first class arrangements for the delivery of the baby at a nearby hospital. I would have a private room and stay in the hospital for ten days.

---

69 The Bartered Bride.

Chapter Fifty-Two
Long Awaited Arrival
Vienna May 23-25, 1952

On Friday, May 23rd Paul accompanied me to the obstetrician. My due date had passed over a week before and there were no signs of impending labor. The doctor recommended we check into the hospital the next day, and if there still was no progress, labor would be induced. They gave me a hot bath and castor oil. That afternoon my water broke and the labor caused a lot of pain, but still no baby. In the evening they sent Paul home, saying they would call him if the baby was born during the night. At 6:00 a.m. Paul called the hospital, only to find out that the baby had still not arrived. Now my husband, as I said, who was passionate about me, the opera and football-I'm not sure in what order- had purchased tickets for an international football match between England and Austria on the first day we arrived in Vienna for himself and his cousin Irwin on May 25 at 2:00 p.m. When Paul arrived at the hospital that morning, he took one look at me and said, "I am calling Irwin." He picked up the telephone on the nightstand next to my bed and I heard him say into the receiver, "If this baby isn't here by lunchtime, you are not going to the football match!"

Irwin arrived at the hospital within the hour, quite calm and composed and told Paul to go visit with his friend, Hans Furth, who lived near the hospital and had returned to Vienna to study medicine. Around noon, Irwin arrived at Hans' apartment in a jovial mood and said, "Let's grab a bite at the coffee house next door."

"What? How is Shirley? Has the baby arrived?" Paul inquired anxiously.

"Just a little more time. We can have lunch first and then return to the hospital," Irwin replied.

Irwin, as was often true, was correct. At 12:45 p.m. Abraham Max Hoffmann, weighing more than eight pounds, entered this world.

Paul kissed my drenched forehead. "Well done! We have a son. He's beautiful!"

He stood over the bassinet and stroked Abe's head. "Welcome! You didn't make this easy for your mother, but it was well worth the wait!"

I had already begun to doze off, when I heard Paul say to Irwin, "First telegraph office to inform the family in Israel and America, then plenty of time to arrive at the stadium for the kick-off!"

CHAPTER FIFTY-THREE
New Mom
Connecticut 2003

"No!" Cara exclaimed. "Papa did not go to a soccer game the day Uncle Abe was born!"

"Yes, he did. Are you surprised? Has anything ever stopped your grandfather from doing what he planned to do throughout his life?" I replied.

"But you just had a baby! It was a difficult birth. Weren't you upset that he left you to go to a soccer game of all things?"

"No. It was a different time; not like today when husbands are in the delivery room and assist with births. And I was exhausted. I'm not even sure that I knew Papa had left. I may have been sedated. I'm sure I slept for several hours. When I awoke later in the afternoon, the nurse who had stayed with me through the night was standing at the foot of the bed with a huge slice of sachertorte, the famous Austrian chocolate cake. Austria is a Catholic country and it was a big deal that Abe was born on Sunday."

"Madame, to celebrate the birth of your son on this blessed day," the nurse said in her best English as she propped me up with some pillows and presented me with the cake. I hadn't eaten in close to forty-eight hours and I'm sure this was not the first thing I should have put into an empty stomach. The smell alone made me queasy. But I felt I had to eat it. She had been so kind and supportive. To this day the smell of chocolate cake brings back vivid memories of that day. By the time Papa got back, soaking wet, I think it rained the entire day, and the Austrian team lost, he was exhausted too. He took one more look at Abe, gave me a kiss and fell on to the bed that was made up for him and slept through the night. I stayed in the hospital for ten days".

"Why ten days? Were you sick?" Cara asked.

"No, that's just the way it was back then. It was nice to be pampered.

"Did Papa stay with you the whole time?"

"No, he visited everyday and spent time getting ready to bring Abe home to the Vienna apartment, our temporary home. Now we could get serious about making plans to go to America. Even though Vienna was where he was born, Papa hated being in Vienna. He could not accept that the people who had been his neighbors for the first eighteen years of his life so readily welcomed the Germans on the day of the Anschluss and the subsequent treatment of the Jewish people. He said the Nazis lurked in the woodwork. Papa went to settle some business on properties his grandfather had left him and his cousins. Thankfully, he was able to reclaim the apartments. He told me he felt the officials and people involved looked at him as if they were thinking, "Why did this Jew survive?"

"How awful," Cara said.

"We needed a birth certificate for Abe so we could obtain a visa for him. Let me tell you what happened when Papa went to register Abe's birth.

Chapter Fifty-Four
Austrian?
Vienna May 26, 1952 - July 1952

On Monday, May 26th, after having breakfast with me in my hospital room, Paul said, "I am going home to shower and change my clothes. I need to go to City Hall and register Abe's birth. We have applied for two visas and now there are three of us. There is no doubt that Abe is Austrian. After all, he was born here. I hope the quota allows for another Austrian to enter the United States this year."

I wasn't surprised that I didn't see Paul again until much later that afternoon. At about 4:00 p.m. he burst into the hospital room, startling me. I had been napping, having just called the nurse to return Abe to the nursery after his afternoon feeding.

Without saying "Hello", he broke into a rant.

"You won't believe the day I just had! Bureaucracy can only be run by idiots!"

Paul was clearly agitated by the events of the day, so I just let him continue. He hardly took a breath.

"I arrived at City Hall just as everyone appeared to be returning from lunch. As I approached the reception desk, I informed the young woman that I was there to register the birth of my son. She offered her congratulations and directed me to an office three doors down the hallway on the right. A bespectacled middle-aged man in a somewhat rumpled brown suit motioned me to take a seat in a chair opposite his desk. He spoke with a French accent so I offered a *"bon jour"*.

"You speak French?" he queried, with a puzzled look. "Yes, I studied and taught at the French Jesuit University in Shanghai." That day the official was French because the Allies still maintained a schedule of rotating control over Vienna, even seven years after the end of the War.

"You'd think this connection would have earned me some degree of understanding if not compassion, but a bureaucrat is a bureaucrat. Upon examining the papers I presented him, including our *Ketubah*,[70] his response was that Austrian law does not recognize religious marriage."

"I then presented our Chinese marriage certificate. His argument this time was that the ceremony had not been performed by a civilian authority. My explanation of Judge Allman's service in the Shanghai Municipal Court apparently did not satisfy his criteria. Partially in an attempt to be witty, but also searching for a solution for this dilemma, I said, "Well I have married my wife twice, if necessary, I will marry her again here in Vienna under Austrian law. But now he had another argument!"

"Well, that would be all well and good, but your wife is a Soviet citizen and under Soviet law, she could not marry a foreigner."

"Can you imagine this ridiculous conversation?" Paul asked.

"Furthermore, he said that the Soviet officials would be in charge the following week and there would be 'ramifications',

---

[70] Jewish marriage contract.

whatever that means, if they saw a marriage between a Soviet citizen and an Austrian."

I stared at Paul in disbelief. There was not a single document anywhere that indicated that I was a Soviet citizen. My birth certificate was issued by the Jewish community and clearly indicated that I was born in Harbin, China. The only relic of my being Russian was my maiden name. How could that carry so much weight?

"I was having a difficult time controlling my temper at this point," Paul said. "I knew I needed to register Abe's birth to obtain an American visa for him. I managed to stay calm, but I think the official began to see my upset. He finally accepted that the Chinese marriage certificate was valid under Austrian law and issued Abe a birth certificate. Our son is now a legitimate Austrian citizen!"

Chapter Fifty-Five
Back to Italy
May - July 1952

Springtime in Vienna was lovely. Tree-lined streets and parks were available for strolling. Most days were warm, but having spent every summer of my life so far in China, what a relief it was to be spared the stifling heat and humidity of crowded streets.

Our sometimes cranky baby was a joy nonetheless. We forgave him our sleepless nights when he looked at us with his large blue eyes that reminded us of the color of the Mediterranean. He was always hungry! Having Irwin and his wife Grete nearby to advise and counsel us on the trials and tribulations of new parenthood provided tremendous support. Irwin had become a father figure to Paul. Whether it was asking medical advice or going to the football games together, it seemed Paul turned to Irwin with the same love and respect that he had for his father. With Grete by my side, my Austrian culinary skills improved dramatically. Now that the baby had arrived, and as idyllic as the time in Vienna seemed, I could tell that Paul was becoming anxious about our next big move, America.

The first week in July arrived and there was no news of our visas. Paul woke up one morning and announced, "I am going to visit the Consulate in Genoa to check on the status of our visa applications."

Two days later I received an excited phone call from Paul. "Start packing," he shouted into the phone. The Consulate says our papers are almost ready. I need to bring you and the baby to Genoa. There will be more interviews."

This is not what I expected to hear, but of course this is what we wanted. Since Paul had left for Genoa, it was the first time I had to take care of Abe on my own and I was exhausted! I tried to generate some excitement to this sudden news.

"That's wonderful news," I exclaimed. "When will you be back?" I asked.

"I am going apartment-hunting today. I'll call you as soon as I find something and catch the next train back to Vienna."

By the end of the week, Paul was back in Vienna and a flurry of activity ensued. It seemed like all the things we needed for Abe were three times as much as what we needed to pack for ourselves. Paul had found an apartment for us in Nervi, the lovely port town on the Italian Riviera we visited a few months earlier; he thought it would be too expensive for our limited budget.

"The rent is reasonable," he told me. "And Nervi will be our home for just a couple of months. But, I'm worried about getting there. The Soviets are currently controlling the borders. I am afraid of another border check and someone assuming you are a Soviet citizen. I am arranging for us to fly to Zurich. From there we can take an overnight train to Milan and then another train to Genoa." This sounded like an arduous journey with a three month old infant, but a reasonable plan nonetheless, and if it was going to minimize Paul's anxiety, it would be worth it.

JEAN HOFFMANN LEWANDA

Abe did not travel well. The flight on British European Airways forty-nine seat *Elizabethan* was less than two hours, but his tiny ears must have been hurting as the plane ascended and descended. Other than in the hospital, Abe had never slept anywhere other than his comfy crib in the quiet backroom in the apartment in Vienna. I was up the entire night rocking him and stifling his cries in an effort not to disturb the other train passengers between Zurich and Genoa. We took a taxi from the train station for the thirty-minute ride to Nervi. It was still early morning when we arrived at the three-story apartment building with a small garden and view of the Mediterranean Sea. The driver helped us with our luggage and I collapsed in an overstuffed armchair with Abe in my arms when we entered the living room.

"Don't you want to see the beautiful view?" Paul asked. "The sea is an incredible shade of blue. There is an orange tree right below our window and the garden is in full bloom.""Not now," I said in a flat expressionless voice. By some miracle, Abe was now sound asleep and I was not going to do anything to change that. I could see the disappointment in Paul's face that I could not express either my enthusiasm or appreciation, but I had not an ounce of energy left in my entire body. I closed my eyes and drifted off.

It must have been an hour or so later when Abe began to stir. When I opened my eyes Paul was standing over Abe and me, holding a cloth diaper and a bottle of warm milk.

"I told the landlord we were coming with a small baby and there was a fresh bottle of milk in the ice box. I'll take Abe now. You look like you would benefit from a warm bath."

I walked down the short hallway to the bathroom and filled the tub. As I slid into the soothing water, I closed my eyes again. This was going to be our home for the next three or four months, or so we thought.

We took the weekend to get settled and Monday morning Paul was back at the Consulate to inform them we were now residing in Italy and to see if there were any further updates. Paul wrote to Judge Allman that evening.

"Dear Judge,

We are now settled in Nervi, a half-hour drive from Genoa. I went to the Consulate today to see how matters have progressed and wish to report to you immediately. The quota stands as follows: they are now working on those who filed before March 1, 1947. I applied on March 4, 1947. Accordingly, our turn should come up in the next quota report, which is in three months. The reception I had at the Consulate was excellent due to your letter. The official in charge of the political section interviewed me for one-and-a-half hours and promised I would get as much consideration as possible. I am sure the case can be considered closed except for the quota number on which nobody can have any influence.

Yours sincerely,

Paul"

So we would be in Italy another three months before we would have any more information on when we would be able to enter the United States of America. If there was anywhere in the world to wait patiently for the next major change in one's life, there was no place better than Nervi.

CHAPTER FIFTY-SIX
An Italian Sojourn
August 1952- November 1952

For the next several months, life on the Italian Riviera normalized, centering around Abe, of course. Paul was becoming restless, not having done any actual work in several months now. He was asked to write a couple of articles about his China experience, which he enjoyed, even doing a broadcast for the Voice of America, which was transmitted throughout Europe and the Far East, and began tutoring a neighbor's children, his natural predilection. He paid $7.00 a month for Italian lessons, rationalizing the expense by saying it never hurt to know another language. Paul did all the food shopping. He relished going to the market several times each week to select from all the fresh fruits and vegetables that were readily available in generous quantities. Meat was still expensive so most nights we ate fresh fish, although we did indulge ourselves a couple of times each week, purchasing either chicken, duck or goose, or an occasional cut of beef. We felt wonderful! Between the sunshine, the cool evening breezes, the healthy diet and the peace and quiet free from political strife, we had found a small slice of heaven on earth and never felt better.

SHALAMA

In early November we received notification that we should report to the United States Consulate. We fully expected that we would be informed that our visas were being processed, we would receive our medical exams and would be on our way to the States before the close of 1952.

We were up early that morning. Abe sucked down his bottle in record time and Paul fed him some crushed bananas as he sat in his high chair, while I readied myself for the half-hour trip to the Consulate.

"Can you believe this?" I called from the bedroom. "Is it possible that today is the day we will finally be granted our visas?"

"I can only hope you are right," Paul said as he propped Abe up on the couch to put on his sweater. The heat of the summer had passed and the nip of fall was in the air.

A few minutes later the three of us, primly dressed, were in a taxi on our way into town to meet with the Consular General. We hardly spoke. The anticipation was palpable. When we entered the consulate, a tall stern looking gentleman stepped out from a previously closed office door.

"Mrs. Hoffmann, could you please come with me." Clearly they were expecting us.

Paul and I gave each other a baffled look. Why would the official just want to speak to me? I placed Abe in Paul's lap and followed the man into his office. He closed the door behind me.

The official positioned an armed chair on the far side of his desk for me. He sat down behind his desk sitting very upright. He opened a thick folder on his desk and after a brief glance at the top page began asking questions.

"Mrs. Hoffmann, where were you born?"

"Harbin, China," I replied.

The official looked up. "Forgive me," he said, "but this is the first time I am interviewing someone with your background. It seems somewhat unusual. What brought your family to Harbin?"

"We are Jewish. There were pogroms in Russia. Jewish boys were being conscripted into the Russian army for twenty-five years. Then the Revolution and the Civil War started. My family was seeking a better life. Harbin offered more economic opportunity and less persecution."

"Did any members of your family have any political affiliations in Harbin or Shanghai?"

"No. We were Zionists. I am the only member of my family who did not emigrate to Israel. If I had not met my husband in 1949, I would be there now."

"What was your father's name?"

"Avram Froloff."

"And where is your father today?"

My father passed away in Israel in November 1951."

"Are you sure?"

I looked at the official in disbelief. "Of course, I am sure. How could anyone not be sure about the death of their father?"

"Are you aware that there is an Avram Froloff living in San Francisco, California. He is a communist union leader. Is he a relation of yours?"

"No, he is not. I have no knowledge of anyone in my father's family. Froloff is a very common Russian name. I am not even certain that my father did not assume this name when he fled Russia in 1919 to avoid military service. Even if there is some family connection, it would be distant. Ashkenazi Jews do not use the same name among the living. We name our children to honor deceased relatives. Hence, my son's name is Abraham, in memory of my deceased father, who, as I said, died in Israel, November 21, 1951."

SHALAMA

The official looked surprised at my rapid and indignant response. Truth be told, I had surprised myself. It was unlike me to speak up to authority figures, but clearly when I felt the need to protect a member of my family, a different side of me emerged, as when Paul was sick in Shanghai. The official made some notes in the folder and closed it with a slow determined motion. I sat silently with my hands folded in my lap. I felt flushed and angry, trying to control my breathing, imagining the upset on my poor departed father's face. He had spent his entire abbreviated life trying to protect me from his hidden past. Now, over a year after his death, someone somewhere had somehow found a way to use his identity to interfere in my life.

The official stood up. "Thank you, Mrs. Hoffmann. I will be sharing this information with our colleagues in Washington, D.C., and will get back to you as soon as they have reviewed it. You may rejoin your husband and son."

I entered the hallway with the official following me. "That will be all for today," the official said. Paul stood up and handed me the baby. "I thought we would be making arrangements to receive our medical clearance today," Paul said.

"I'm sorry. That will have to wait. I need to send your dossier back to Washington for additional review."

"What the hell just happened?" Paul burst out as we stepped outside the Consulate into the cool morning air.

"You are not going to believe this but we are still being plagued by the phantom communist connection!" I exclaimed.

"Now what? Do they think we are spies?" Paul inquired. "It seems like anything is possible at this point."

"I guess. There is a communist in San Francisco with the same name as my father. It was all I could do to try and convince him that my father is dead!"

"Jiminy Cricket!" Paul exclaimed "When will this stop!"

JEAN HOFFMANN LEWANDA

We walked silently to the main thoroughfare and hailed a cab to take us back to Nervi. Due to Senator Joseph McCarthy and his Red Scare, we would be biding our time on the Italian Riviera. Clearly, this wasn't the worst place to be, but once again we were in limbo, far from family with our future postponed. We would have to wait another four months before we would be called back to the Consulate to receive our medical clearance and visas to enter the United States of America.

SHALAMA

CHAPTER FIFTY-SEVEN
Incomprehensible
Connecticut 2003

"I'm trying to understand," said Cara. "I read about the Red Scare in my History of Film classes this semester. It seems hard to believe that anyone would assume that you had any connection to anyone that would make you a danger to this country. You were just looking to be reunited with your family and get on with your life."

"Again, mamela, it was a different time. The War had taken so much from everyone. The focus was on rebuilding and keeping out all forces that might interfere with those goals. Officials were being very careful not to make a mistake. We understood better than most the havoc communist influence could wreak on daily life. Papa would tell you he did not relax about the communist threat until we reached American shores."

"Is it possible that they were also concerned that Papa was a spy?"

"Wouldn't that make our story even more exotic?" I replied with a laugh. "It's true that Judge Allman, Papa's boss in Shanghai, worked for the OSS, the precursor to the CIA, and must have been engaged in some clandestine activities during his many years in China. As far as I can tell you, I don't think Papa did anything that would be defined as espionage. But he did have to follow Judge Allman's directives when it came to shutting down the law firm and their clients, and you know that was very difficult. Did Papa know more than he has told us? Probably, but that is not unusual. Just like my father, certain things were never shared to protect loved ones."

"So what did you do for the next four months in Nervi?" Cara asked.

"More of the same, until the day your Uncle Abe decided we needed just a little more excitement."

Chapter Fifty-Eight
Nervi
November 1952 - April 1953

For the next four months, Abe was our primary distraction as our wait for visas dragged on. He was growing quickly and seemed to be developing and acquiring skills even faster than one would expect. On our evening strolls, people passing by never failed to comment on how alert and beautiful Abe was. He smiled for everyone. No one believed he was only six months old. Our neighbors and friends, some whom we knew from Shanghai and were also awaiting papers to move on to Australia, visited with us regularly and oohed and aahed over our precious bundle. A retired English couple lived in the apartment directly above us and became surrogate grandparents. Colonel Turner-Coles, a towering stately gentleman with a shock of white hair, who had served in the British Military, was jovial and outgoing. Mrs. Turner-Coles was the picture of calm and compassion. The colonel and his wife had no children and it was all they could do to keep themselves from fawning over Abe each and every day. Abe repaid their attention with smiles and giggles. It was truly a delight to watch our infant son interact with this lovely couple as we sat in our courtyard under the orange tree in the Mediterranean sunshine.

One afternoon, I had been sitting on our terrace when I heard Abe stirring in his crib after his nap. I noticed he had thrown his favorite toy, a cat that meowed when you squeezed it, out of his crib. As I picked it up, I noticed that the plastic disc that made the meow sound was missing. I rustled through Abe's blanket and couldn't find it. I picked Abe up and placed him on the floor and he began to cry. "Ssh," I said "I'll pick you up as soon as I find the piece to your toy." When I didn't see it I pulled the sheet off the crib mattress and when I still didn't see it I pulled the mattress out of the crib. My heart began to race. I called out to Paul, who had been sitting in the garden reading. "Ask the Colonel to bring his car around. We need to see a doctor!"

Paul came running up the stairs. "What's wrong? " he asked, surveying the disarrayed room with Abe and the crib linens and mattress on the floor. Are you hurt? Is Abe hurt?"

I proceeded to show him the cat, sans whistle, and said, "I think Abe swallowed it."

"Why would you think that?" Paul asked.

"Because when I left the room so he could take his nap, he had the cat in his mouth."

Paul got down on his hands and knees and ran his hands over the floor. He stood up and shook out the crib linens. The whistle was nowhere to be found.

"Let's not panic. Abe is clearly breathing just fine. If he swallowed it, there should be a gift in his diaper in a day or two."

Two days later, Abe started to cough and his breathing became labored. When we put our ears to his chest we could hear a distinct whistling sound.

"I told you! I told you! I know that he swallowed that whistle!" I cried out in panic.

This time Paul didn't hesitate. He called the Colonel and we were on our way to the pediatrician, a Polish Jew who had come to Italy to study medicine. He immediately sent us to the hospital in Genoa for X-rays. We took everything but Abe's diaper off as we lay him on the table. The radiologist came out to tell us that it was nothing more than a button on the child's clothing.

"A button?" Paul said, "On a naked baby?"

The doctor went back behind the door and this time came back with a diagnosis of an enlarged thymus gland. Over the next couple of days, Abe's condition worsened. When we noticed his lips turning blue, we once again called the Colonel and returned to the hospital. The Colonel took a seat in the waiting room while we carried Abe into the examination room. Once again X-rays were taken with a very different result. The rubber disc had lodged in Abe's esophagus and by this time had caused inflammation that restricted his breathing. The doctor sedated him and successfully removed the disk with a long narrow tweezer and to our huge relief, Abe recovered beautifully. From then on, we said, only half jokingly, "If one gets sick in Italy, the prescription is, "Take the first flight out."

In March, the long-awaited letter came. We were to report to the American Consulate in Genoa once again. Within two weeks we had our medical appointments, received our visas and preparations began in earnest for our trip to what we had begun calling "The Promised Land".

On April 10, 1953, more than thirteen months after our departure from Shanghai, the *SS Homeland* weighed anchor from the port of Genoa.

Chapter Fifty-Nine
The Promised Land
May 1953 - April 1954

US Lines, the client responsible for our delayed departure from Shanghai, kept its promise. As soon as our visas were approved, first class accommodations on the *SS Homeland* were booked. On our two week passage to New York City we learned that the *Homeland* had a storied past. One of the earliest steam turbine ocean liners, launched in 1901, it served as a troopship and patrol boat in World War I and as an evacuation vessel in World War II, surviving near misses by torpedoes while in service. One of the most interesting, or exciting tales in the ship's history was told to us when we were invited one evening to dine at the captain's table, a perk extended to all first class passengers. When done eating, the captain took a sip of wine, pushed his dinner plate to the side, set down his glass directly in front of him and became animated as he began the narrative.

"On April 15, 1912 the *Homeland*, then called the *Virginian*, was in the North Atlantic steaming north, about 200 miles from where the *RMS Titanic* collided with an iceberg. The *Virginian* heard the garbled distress call from the *Titanic* and reversed direction to respond to the SOS," the captain told us.

The entire table of twelve diners fell silent and moved in closer, waiting to hear what role the *Virginian* played in the most famous ship-sinking in nautical history.

"*RMS Carpathia* was the first to arrive on the scene and was able to rescue 705 passengers. The *Virginian* was more than halfway to the wreckage when it received a signal from the *Carpathia* to turn back, that the ice was too closely packed to approach. The *Virginian* ended up passing within six or seven miles of the sinking, but no evidence of the *Titanic,* lifeboats or any other debris were spotted."

"It's an ironic coincidence that this is the ship to bring us to America," Paul commented.

"Why is that?" asked the captain. Everyone at the table listened intently as Paul related the highlights of his journey, which began in Vienna in 1938.

"There is more to tell," said the captain. From 1920 through the late 1940s, Swedish American Lines owned the *Virginian*, renamed the *Drottningholm.* It made many trips across the Atlantic repatriating nationals on both sides of the ocean. There were rescues and prisoner exchanges. The Lubavitcher Rebbe, Rabbi Yosef Yitzchak Schneersohn, then the leader of the Chabad movement, arrived in New York City aboard the *Drottningholm* in 1940 from Gothenburg, Sweden having escaped Riga, Latvia. There were many released from concentration camps that sailed the *Drottningholm* for North and South America. It certainly is serendipitous, Paul," concluded the captain. "This vessel did it all, serving as a warship, but also providing humanitarian aid. In fact, Drottningholm earned the nickname *Rollinghome.* I hope that this ship, now called the *Homeland,* foreshadows what lies ahead for you and your family," he said.

All I could think when the captain said that was, "From your mouth to God's ears." For me it had been thirteen months of exile. For Paul it had been thirteen years.

The captain raised his glass to offer a toast and all the diners followed suit. "Smooth sailing to old and new homes, wherever they may be!"

Chapter Sixty
Out of Exile
Connecticut 2003

"You know mamela, what we felt when we saw the Statue of Liberty on the morning of April 26, 1953? It was incredible! We stood at the railing on the deck, Papa holding Abe in his arms. He said to me, "Can you believe it? We made it!" There was nothing else to say.

Oma Lili, your great-grandmother, was waiting at the pier. After a quick meeting with Judge Allman, we were on a train to Utica, New York, where Papa's father had a position at the state hospital."

"I remember Oma," Cara said. "She died when I was eight years old. I can still hear her German accent. She always had M&Ms for us when we came to visit."

"Opa Oskar was at the train station with Papa's cousin Fred when we arrived in Utica.

Papa was overcome with emotion when he saw his father. Opa had suffered a heart attack in the Wildflecken Displaced Persons Camp in Bavaria where they were waiting for their visas for months after leaving Shanghai. Papa feared he might not see his father again. As happy as I was to see all of Papa's relatives, I also experienced a strange jealousy knowing I would never see my father again.

JEAN HOFFMANN LEWANDA

It would be another seven years before we brought my mother to this country, eight years until my brother came and nine years before we traveled to California so I could visit with my aunt and cousins."

"There was another irony about the boat that brought us to America. We were on one of the SS Homeland's last voyages. After fifty-four years of sailing the seas, the ship returned to Genoa and was scrapped in 1955 after all those years of incredible journeys through the turmoil and chaos that was the 20th Century. As it had been for us, the SS Homeland arrived at its last port of call."

"But it must have been somewhat tumultuous and chaotic getting settled in America too," said Cara. "It's not like you had been there before and knew what to expect."

"That's true," said Shalama. "One more story before we call it quits for today."

Chapter Sixty-One
Jeanie
April 17, 1954

By July, Paul had found a job with a trademark firm in New York City that had done work with Allman, Kops and Lee in Shanghai. They were willing to hire him while he went to law school and studied for the bar exam. He went to Brooklyn Law School four nights each week for three years. His European high school education, his Aurora University degree and six years of work experience as a lawyer in Shanghai earned him the equivalent of one year of credit towards his law degree. We rented a two bedroom garden apartment in the Flushing section of Queens, New York and began life as we would know it for the next several years.

With all the changes in our lives, it didn't seem strange to me that I did not have a period in August. There were many sleepless nights with Abe struggling to adjust to a different environment once again. It didn't even occur to me in September that I might be pregnant since my period was often irregular and I had grown to expect to be tired a good portion of the time while setting up a household with a toddler underfoot. By the first week in October,

I asked a Shanghai friend, who also lived in Queens, if she knew of an obstetrician.

"You are not going to believe this," my friend Goldie said. "Do you remember Dr. Mindlin from Harbin?"

"I remember that name," I replied. "That was the Jewish doctor at the Jewish Hospital where everyone's babies were delivered. If I am not mistaken, he delivered my brother and me!"

The following week, Dr. Mindlin confirmed that, yes, I was pregnant. Since Paul was swamped with the responsibilities of work and law school, I hadn't mentioned that I had a doctor's appointment. We had not planned on having another child just yet, and I didn't want to worry him unnecessarily until I was sure I had some good news to share.

It was all I could do to force myself to stay awake on October 14, 1953. It was Paul's 33rd birthday. It was a Wednesday night and Paul wasn't going to be home from law school until after 10:00 p.m.. He usually found me under the covers sound asleep when he came home. That night, I greeted him at the door with a kiss. I took his briefcase and jacket out of his hands, placed them on a chair and placed his hand on my belly.

"Happy Birthday!" I said.

Paul stared at me in disbelief. "Impossible!" he said. "It took over a year to conceive Abe. We weren't even trying! When is this baby due?"

"Early April," I responded.

"A wonderful time to have a baby," Paul whispered in my ear as we embraced.

Unfortunately, Dr. Mindlin did not believe the advice I had received after Abe's birth in Vienna. The doctor there told me that if I was to have another baby, labor should be induced close to my due date. Dr. Mindlin's response to this was, "The Chinese women squat in the rice paddy and deliver their babies. This is a second baby. You'll be fine." Once again my due date came and went with no signs of labor. Should I have mentioned to Dr. Mindlin that there were no rice paddies in Flushing, Queens? Passover was approaching and I was vigorously cleaning and cooking. Paul tried to dissuade me from putting in so much effort since he was certain that I would be too busy caring for a newborn to be concerned about observing the holiday. The day before the first Seder my water broke, but no labor pains. Paul took me to Kew Gardens Hospital where upon hearing that my water had broken, I was immediately admitted. After almost two days in the hospital, Paul called Dr. Mindlin. "I am worried," he told the doctor. "Shirley's water broke early yesterday morning."

There was a long pause at the other end of the line. "I didn't realize it had been that long," the doctor replied. "I am worried too," Dr. Mindlin said without disguising the concern in his voice. "I'll meet you at the hospital," he told Paul.

At 7:45 p.m. on April 17, 1954, as the rest of the family participated in the first Seder, Jean Gilda entered the world by forceps delivery. My father-in-law Oskar commented, "This baby is smart. She knew that this world can be a difficult place. She preferred to stay where it was safe and warm."

CHAPTER SIXTY-TWO
Passing the Torch
Connecticut 2003

"I think I've told you everything," said Shalama. "There are no more stories to tell."

"That can't be," disagreed Cara. "You were only 24 when you left China and twenty-six years old when Mom was born here in America. What about the next fifty years?"

"You make a good point, mamela. In those twenty-four years in China, ninety-six seasons, there were a lifetime of changes. But, what happened in the next fifty years, is what happens to everyone. You work hard, you watch your children grow, you get a bigger home, parents become ill, parents die, maybe you move, children marry, grandchildren are born. Papa and I had all of this. Were there rough patches? Of course there were. Any tragedy or sadness-and we were not unscathed-could not overshadow the amount of joy and good fortune with which we were blessed. It will be up to your Mom to share the stories of her lifetime. My job is done."

Cara could see the fatigue in her grandmother's eyes. She switched off the tape recorder that had captured the incredible events of Shalama's life.

SHALAMA

"Your stories were wonderful, Amma. Now they are my stories too. Can I get you something before I go," asked Cara, kissing her grandmother on the forehead.

"No, mamela. I think I will just sit here for a little while and rest before dinner."

Cara saw Shalama's eyes close as she quietly closed the door to the apartment.

Chapter Sixty-Three
The Last Adventure
Connecticut 2012

The two years since Paul's passing had been quiet and sad for Shalama. Her children and grandchildren surrounded her with love and attention, but Paul's death had left a void that could not be filled. He passed away in March of 2010. He had been stricken with Parkinson's disease two years earlier, spending the last several weeks of his life mostly bedridden, unable to speak, his only communication being long stares with his still remarkably clear warm brown eyes. Shalama missed him terribly and although she went to bed each night always remarking, "Tomorrow is another day," she felt herself slipping away. When asked the day or date, she often erred. Was it really that important? Did it make a difference what day it was? Did it matter what happened yesterday? Or what would happen tomorrow?

Shalama's daughter, Jeanie, stopped by the assisted living facility most days, if only for a few minutes in the late afternoon, after her busy day teaching children with special needs at a nearby elementary school. On this day, something in Jeanie's usually calm demeanor was different. After the quick peck on the cheek and the routine "How are you?" that would be answered with "How could I be?," Jeanie positioned herself on

SHALAMA

a chair opposite Shalama's recliner so that they were face to face.

"Mom, does the name George Frolov mean anything to you?"

"George, who?"

"Frolov. Almost like your maiden name, just spelled with a 'v' instead of 'ff'."

"No. I never met or heard of another Froloff in my entire life."

"When Abe got back to his office this afternoon, after what he said was a harrowing day in court, he took a phone call from a man with a heavy Russian accent claiming to be your first cousin. He has been living here in Farmington, less than five miles away, for the last thirty-four years. Abe was rattled, had something pressing he had to do related to what had happened in court that morning, and didn't even get George's phone number. Abe called me at the end of the day, obviously upset, to tell me about this call. I did an internet search and yes, there is a George Frolov in Farmington. I found a phone number. Do you want me to call him?"

Shalama placed her hand on her chest over her heart and gasped. "It's not possible! After all these years! And so close! Someone from Papa's family in Nevel...the family he left behind... Yes, please, call!"

Jeanie took out her cell phone, put it on speaker and dialed the number. The accent of the deep voice on the other end was unmistakable. Jeanie briefly explained that she was Abe's sister and had heard about their encounter earlier in the day. Upon hearing George's voice, Shalama immediately began speaking to him in Russian. Her eyes began to well up. She handed the phone back to Jeanie. Jeanie arranged to meet George and his wife, Sima, with Shalama in a local restaurant two days later for lunch.

A little before noon that Wednesday, Shalama's aide escorted her to the car. Claire had made her usual effort to ensure Shalama was well dressed and groomed. Claire whispered "Good luck, Mrs. Hoffmann" as she gave Jeanie a knowing nod and helped Shalama adjust her seat belt. "Your Mom has talked of nothing else but her father since that *phone call, even in her sleep. Let's hope that this is the connection that has been missing all these many years."*

When Shalama and Jeanie arrived at the restaurant, a fashionably dressed couple in their 70s were already seated at a table towards the rear of the room. Jeanie pushed chairs out of the way so that Shalama could maneuver her walker to where George and Sima were sitting. After exchanging greetings in Russian, there was a moment where George and Shalama stared at each other's faces, searching for some long lost familial resemblance.

George began his story. He and Sima and their twelve-year-old daughter, Tatiana, had arrived in Baltimore in 1979, with the first wave of Soviet Jewish immigrants. Both engineers, and unhappy in Baltimore, by 1980 they found jobs in their fields near Hartford, Connecticut and settled in with the relatively large Russian Jewish community in West Hartford.

"Oh my God," exclaimed Shalama. "If you had come to the Bridgeport area we would've met thirty years ago!" As soon as the Soviet Jewish refugees had begun arriving, Shalama had volunteered to help with their resettlement. Her Russian was still fluent and she was by their side, at doctor's appointments, in childbirth classes, at the motor vehicle department, to serve as a translator and advocate. Within no time at all, Shirley and Paul had an extended family, who visited often, sharing meals, and simchas[71]. They were able to offer legal advice and assist with finding employment.

How many had been there for them as they had traveled and resettled around the world? It not only felt natural, it was joyful to be in the position of those that helped them find freedom and stability in their new homeland. If the Soviet Jews had stayed in the Soviet Union they would always be identified as Jews, forever stuck in jobs with no future, forever sharing single rooms with their parents and children.

---

[71] Celebrations.

SHALAMA

One apartment might house eight or nine families with a single kitchen and toilet. There would be toilet seats hanging from nails on the wall, each one designated for one family. To bathe, they would have to visit the public bath house.

George continued. "I retired last year and now had time to follow up on some questions my family has had for years; but before the Internet, there was no good way to find answers. My father was one of five brothers and two sisters that we knew about. There was a story that floated around among the aunts and uncles about an older brother, an eighth sibling, who went to China around the time of the Revolution. We believe his name was Avram."

Shalama was about to take a sip of water, but put down her glass as her hand began to shake. "My father's name was Avram. And I was born in Harbin. I don't know exactly when my father arrived, I think around 1919, but my parents were married in January of 1924."

"When I began searching for Avram Frolov on the Internet," said George, "I started with the premise that if he had come to America he might have changed his name to Abraham, and it would not be unusual for the spelling of Frolov to be changed to Froloff. When I found you in the white pages, saw your maiden name was Froloff and had a son named Abraham, I had to make the connection. It was easy to find the phone number for your son's law practice."

"My father never came to America. When my parents left China in February 1951, they went to Israel. Papa died there in November of 1951. I was already pregnant with my son who was born the following May. Of course, we gave him my father's name, but anglicized it to Abraham. My mother-in-law asked us why we gave him such a Jewish name. My husband asked her if she ever heard of Abraham Lincoln!"

"The hunt for your father started a couple of years ago," said George. "The Russian government decided it wanted to honor airmen who had gone down during World War II and provide a proper burial. The United States had lent the Russians fighter planes in 1943 in hopes of expediting the end of the War. Officials began combing the countryside, talking to local residents about their memories of the War. When they arrived in Brest in Belarus, a group of men told the officials they witnessed the crash of an aircraft when they were boys. They took the officials out into a field and indicated the spot. A crew was brought to the site and began digging. Seven meters underground they found the remains of an aircraft and its crew. They found the personal effects of David Frolov with identifying information that could connect him with his family. The authorities posted this information on the Internet and David's son, Eduard, was found living in St. Petersburg, Russia, now about eighty-five years old. Eduard has a daughter, Olga, who is a librarian in academia. She was the one who contacted me for help in finding the 'mystery' uncle," said George.

"This is all very interesting but my father never mentioned any brothers or sisters specifically, but he did say there were babies at home when he left. The time frame fits but how can we be sure? We always thought Papa had changed his name to sound more Russian, to distance himself from whomever he left behind. You know that the Soviets came into Harbin as late as 1945, still looking for deserters. But we were long gone. We went to Shanghai in 1940."

"It is unusual for Jews to have the name Frolov," replied George. "There's a database of all the Jews who served in the Soviet Army in World War II. Every Frolov listed is a member of our family. We know that we have had the name for at least four generations. Our great-grandfather served in a military Canton. By order of the Czar, each Canton had to acquire fifty new 'recruits' each year. These were often poor or orphaned boys around the age of twelve who were taken into service for twenty to twenty-five years. It's possible that our ancestor somehow acquired the Frolov name at that time."

"This all sounds possible, but how can we know for sure?" asked Shalama.

After listening quietly to the exchange between George and Shalama,

SHALAMA

Jeanie interjected, "Mom, we have so many photographs, many of the subjects you can identify, many of whom you can't, and some photos have no inscription on the back. I think we should ask George and Sima to come over for dinner on Sunday and maybe the photographs will offer some clues."

A few days later, George arrived at Jeanie's home to find the dining room table covered from end to end with old photographs. It didn't take but a moment for George to go around the table pointing to individual pictures reciting out loud, "my uncle, my aunt, my uncle, my aunt, my grandfather, and my father!" He lowered his glasses on his nose to take a closer look at the portrait of a handsome young man in uniform, posed with his head slightly turned, as if looking off into the distance. "My God!" George exclaimed. "I have never seen a picture of my father so young!"

Shalama had been sitting in the armchair at the end of the table. Tears began to stream down her cheeks. George pulled up a chair beside her and they embraced.

"All these years, an entire lifetime, I never knew. Seven brothers and sisters! How many cousins? What happened to them all? Where are they now?"

"There is so much to tell," said George.

"Why the secrecy? How could Papa not tell us? How many hearts were broken when he left, never to return?"

George cleared an area of the dining room table and opened a three-ring binder he had brought with him. "Let me introduce you to your family." George had scanned some photographs from his collection and enlarged them on letter-size paper.

The very first page was a photo of an ancient looking elderly couple.

All color drained from Shalama's face. "I know this picture. Who are these people? When we first came to Shanghai, there was a letter. This picture fell out. Papa put it in his coat pocket."

"You didn't ask him about it?" asked George.

"No," replied Shalama. "We could tell from the look on his face that this was something he did not want to share."

"These are your grandparents, Solomon and Sarah Frolov."

"We knew our grandfather's name was Solomon because Papa would sign his patronymic name, Avram Solomonovich Froloff, but I never knew my grandmother's name."

"Solomon and Sarah were relocated to the Soviet Gorky Province to escape the German occupation," said George. "Sarah died there in 1941 at the age of sixty-three. Solomon returned to Nevel when the war ended. Your father's brothers, David, Reuven and Moises were casualties of war, losing their lives fighting for Mother Russia. My father, Michael, also served in the military, but as a doctor. We were stationed in Vladivostok, not all that far from Harbin. A neighbor in Nevel wrote to my father asking for money because Solomon had no means of support and was starving. He passed away before help arrived. He was seventy years old. This is very likely the last picture taken of them before Sarah's death in '41. Boris, and Michael, my father, survived the War and went on to have families. Galena and Zinaida, the only girls, went on to be strong Soviet supporters, as were Boris and Michael. There was a brief period of time when it looked like there would be a better life for Jews in Russia, where they would be treated as equals, but that did not last very long."

"So, why did my father leave? What did he want that the others did not?"

"Our grandfather, Solomon, was a very religious man. He spent most days studying Torah. Sarah kept a garden and Solomon brought in some income by driving a dray and tending cattle. Your father was the oldest and he often studied with his father. That is the only education he had, but from his handwriting on the back of these old photographs, he appears to be an educated man. I have to think his faith and heritage was important to him and maybe this was his impetus. Not a single member of the family maintained their Jewish practices. When World

SHALAMA

War II started, the Soviets eliminated all aspects of organized Jewish life. Many died fighting for the Soviet Army, including the three Frolov brothers. Many more died in the 900 day German siege of Leningrad.[72] *Today some of our relatives have no connection with Judaism at all,"* replied George.

"*Papa raised Teva and I to be very proud of being Jewish. We observed all the holidays, We went to Jewish Schools. Teva became a bar mitzvah. We were Zionists. We participated in Betar, a Zionist youth group with militaristic leanings. We were all going to Israel. Mama, Papa and Teva made Aliyah. If I hadn't met my husband, Paul, in Shanghai before we were scheduled to leave, I more than likely would be in Israel today.*"

"*And this may have been what made your father sever all ties with his family,*" said George.

---

[72] St. Petersburg was renamed Leningrad under the Soviets.

Chapter Sixty-Four
A Sweet Goodbye
August 8, 2012

Cara and her mom, Jeanie, stood side-by-side, holding their beloved Amma's hands as she took her last breath. It had been just four short months since George had found Shalama and revealed a lifetime of mysteries. Cara and Jeanie embraced, releasing soft sobs, both realizing that there would be no more stories, that an incredible mother and grandmother was gone.

"Mom," said Cara, "Amma was so strong. She accepted all that life dealt her with the same grace and resilience, regardless of the risk and outcome."

"Yes, she was a humble heroine. When she related her incredible stories, one never sensed she felt she had done anything extraordinary. But, you couldn't help but feel that she was just a little bit proud of her adventurous spirit! She loved sharing all she had seen and done. Her love and respect for people of all cultures was just one of her many gifts. Amma was a rare individual who appreciated all that life offered.

"We cherish any small part of Amma that lives within us. May her memory be a blessing."

Afterword

The lives of the Jewish Community of Harbin, China has been documented and preserved by Professor Dan Ben-Canaan, who has coined his own moniker, "The Only Jew in Harbin." Dan has worked with the Chinese government to restore three Jewish landmarks in Harbin. The Harbin Jewish School is now a music conservatory, the Old Synagogue is a concert hall, and the New Synagogue is a museum. Dan's research archive, which includes photos of the matzah factory where my grandmother helped make the Passover matzah, a family funeral circa 1925, the family in front of the apartment house on Bolotnaia Ulitsa, and my mom and uncle in their school uniforms, is housed at the YIVO Institute in New York City. Some of the missing pieces to the mystery of the Froloff/Egudkin family have been locked up in an archive in Beijing since 1985. While the government of Heilongjiang Province supported Dan in the restoration of the three aforementioned sites, presumably to encourage tourism, they would not allow access to records that could document the arrival and land records of the Jewish residents of Harbin, presumably so descendants could not request restitution. When I first started communicating with Dan in 2016, he asked me for a power of attorney, which I provided, to see if a legal document would help gain access to the archive, but to no avail.

I know my grandmother arrived in Harbin by train in 1917 as a young girl with her parents, one brother, and three sisters. Her birth certificate was lost somewhere on that journey. I have notarized Israeli immigration documents, attestations by my grandmother's aunt and uncle that she was born in 1903 in

Novozibkov, and they know this to be true because "they are Fanya's aunt and uncle and they were present at her birth." I presumed that my grandfather came on his own sometime after his eighteenth birthday.

Other life cycle events in Harbin were recorded by the Jewish Community and I have documents for the marriage, birth, and death of members of my mother's family; including the record of my uncle's circumcision.

The mystery of Avram and his family was truly a mystery. My mother did mention that there was some communication to Avram's family through Fanya's family, but she never knew anything about her father's family, and truth be told she died without knowing. George Frolov contacted us two years after my mother's passing. He had searched the Internet for Abraham Froloff and the very first entry was my mom's obituary, *Shulamis Froloff, daughter of Abraham and Fanya Froloff*. I took license to include the story George brought us before her passing because I can only imagine the emotional impact this revelation would have had on my Mom.

In the course of writing this book the mystery only became more intriguing. Through my amazing contacts at *Historic Shanghai*, Tina Kanagaratnam and Patrick Cranley, previously unknown information came funneling in. Tina put me in touch with Katya Knyazeva, a research fellow at the University of the Eastern Piedmont, in Vercelli, Italy, who provided additional information. Katya referred me to the Kharbarovsk Archive (BREM-Bureau of Russians Emigres to Manchuria) where she had discovered a eleven-page file on my grandfather, Avram, as well as information on my great grandmother, Golda Riva Estrin Egudkin. My cousin Olga Frolovna in St. Petersburg, Russia, granddaughter of one of Avram's seven siblings, David Frolov, was able to access the Kharbarovsk Archive. It was from this archive that I finally discovered some details of my grandfather's early life. Avram never attended school, arrived in Harbin in 1919, declared himself a Monarchist, had a kiosk selling milk in the bazaar and applied for permission to go to Shanghai in the fall of 1939. Eli Kharaz provided the translation and interpretation of these documents. Eli, his wife Katarina, and their two children, Vadim and Anna, were one of the several Soviet Jewish families that Shirley and Paul helped settle in Connecticut. Eli and Katarina provided the insights I needed to depict Russian Jewish family life.

Most of the events included in the book are based on the oral history my mother told throughout the course of her lifetime. Over the years, friends of my parents have documented their extraordinary life experience and I have combed through their writings to find places and events that corroborate with the stories my mother shared with me. Another valuable resource was *The Bulletin*, published until 2021 by an organization called *Igud Yotzei Sin*, Former Jewish Residents of Shanghai. Over the span of close to forty years, the Jewish communities of Harbin, Tientsin and Shanghai, although spread across the world, predominantly in Israel, the United States and Australia, kept in touch. It was through *The Bulletin* that I learned about the lives of some of the key players in this story such as Rabbi Aharon Kiselev and Dr. Abraham Kaufman.

The publication of *Witness to History: From Vienna to Shanghai*, my father's memoir led to several speaking engagements throughout the Eastern United States. It was not unusual for someone in the audience to approach me to share that friends or relatives, or they too, were former residents of China. Following a presentation in Scotch Plains, New Jersey in November of 2023 a gentleman told me he was born in Harbin and also lived in Shanghai. Not only did he share my mother's background, he was a classmate of my mother's brother, Teva, at the Shanghai Jewish School. George Tomkins, known in China as Grigori Levovich Tomchinsky, shared his memories, several which have been incorporated in this story,

The details and conversations of the intimate life of my mother's family are the product of my imagination, stories that I was able to elaborate on, often because of some artifact that surfaced that could help substantiate what may have been the truth. Examples of this are the brass candlesticks that were identified by an antiques dealer as Russian, mid-1800's and the bolt of gray worsted pin striped wool I found in a carved Chinese chest that traveled from Shanghai to Israel to Los Angeles to Connecticut that my mother said was intended for a suit for her brother. Many of the events of the 1950's contain actual quotes, words that both my parents wrote in letters to their relatives and my father's employer, Norwood Allman. I have also taken the liberty of quoting Judge Allman verbatim from his letters to my father. An extensive archive of Norwood Allman's papers exists at the Hoover Institute on the campus of Stanford University in Palo Alto, California. I found two pieces of correspondence between my father and Judge Allman included in this archive. The archive includes an incredible amount of information on the Judge's dealings within China throughout his lifetime, as well as declassified documents related to his OSS activities. My examination of the archive substantiated many of the events surrounding the experience of lawyers after the communists took control of Shanghai.

This is a story that would not have been a story without the historical context of time in which it took place. I made every effort to document the events of history as accurately as possible from the perspective of my mother, her family and friends. I apologize for any inaccuracies that may appear in the text. I only wish that these brave and loving people were still with us to tell their stories first-hand.

Acknowledgements

Although writing at first seemed to be a lonely task, I soon discovered this was not true. Through the creation of this manuscript, I have spent so many hours with people I have loved, reliving their past, and it has been tremendously joyful as well as incredibly heart wrenching. Also, both old and new friends have given selflessly of their time, providing feedback that has guided me through my first fictional work. I owe tremendous thanks to Robin Schwartz, Susan Blumberg-Kason, Diana Newman, Andrea Thayer, Lisa King, Barry Lipnick, Katarina Kharaz, Carolyn Olsen and Jodi Lewanda for their thoughtful review of the manuscript. I listened carefully to all their comments and did my best to integrate their suggestions. Special thanks to Tina Kanagaratnam and Patrick Cranley for providing photos of where Shalama lived in Shanghai as well as a treasure trove of information that supported Shalama's story. If it weren't for Tina and Patrick I may never have connected with Katya Knyazeva who discovered my grandfather's file in the Khabarovsk Archive. I will be forever grateful to Katya as well.

A special note of thanks to my mother's first cousin, George Frolov. It was George's efforts to solve the mystery of the older brother that went to China that brought Avram's story to light. I must also thank Olga Frolovna, our cousin in St. Petersburg, Russia, granddaughter of David Frolov, for her tireless efforts to gain access to the Khabarovsk Archive.

The perspectives and information provided by Eli Kharaz, from his translation of the BREM file from Khabarovsk, and George Tomkins with his personal stories of the Shanghai Jewish

School, were invaluable. These were insights which would never have been available to me without their assistance. I believe this information brought both depth and color to the story and I am thankful for the opportunity to learn from them.

Many thanks to Victoria Graham for her help editing this manuscript. Looking at the text through Victoria's lens was both enlightening and instructive.

A special note of thanks to Graham Earnshaw and Earnshaw Books for bringing the unique experience of Jewish communities in China to a worldwide audience. Graham's willingness to publish both *Witness to History: From Vienna to Shanghai* and *Shalama: My 96 Seasons in China* has come at a time when these stories need to be told.

The support of my children, David and Cara, my daughter-in-law Erica, my grandchildren, Jonathan and Alexis, and my brother Abe, has added satisfaction to the re-imagining of my mother's experiences. I hope that they enjoy the time they will be able to spend with their mother, grandmother and great-grandmother when reading her story.

Jean Hoffmann Lewanda
February 2024

JEAN HOFFMANN LEWANDA

Teva, Fanya and Shalama - First day of Harbin Russian School circa 1938

SHALAMA

Shalama and Teva - Summer on the Sugari circa 1938 - Harbin

WEDDING HOFFMANN-FROLOFF

On Sunday, March 5, the wedding of Miss S. Froloff and Mr. P. A. Hoffmann took place at the Oheil Moishe Synagogue. Picture shows from left to right: Mr. and Mrs. A. S. Froloff, the bride's parents; the bride and groom; Dr. and Mrs. O. Hoffmann, the groom's parents. After the ceremony a cocktail reception was held at the Masonic Temple, attended by about 250 friends and well-wishers of the young couple.— Lacks News Photo.

Wedding Announcement March 5, 1950 - Shanghai

JEAN HOFFMANN LEWANDA

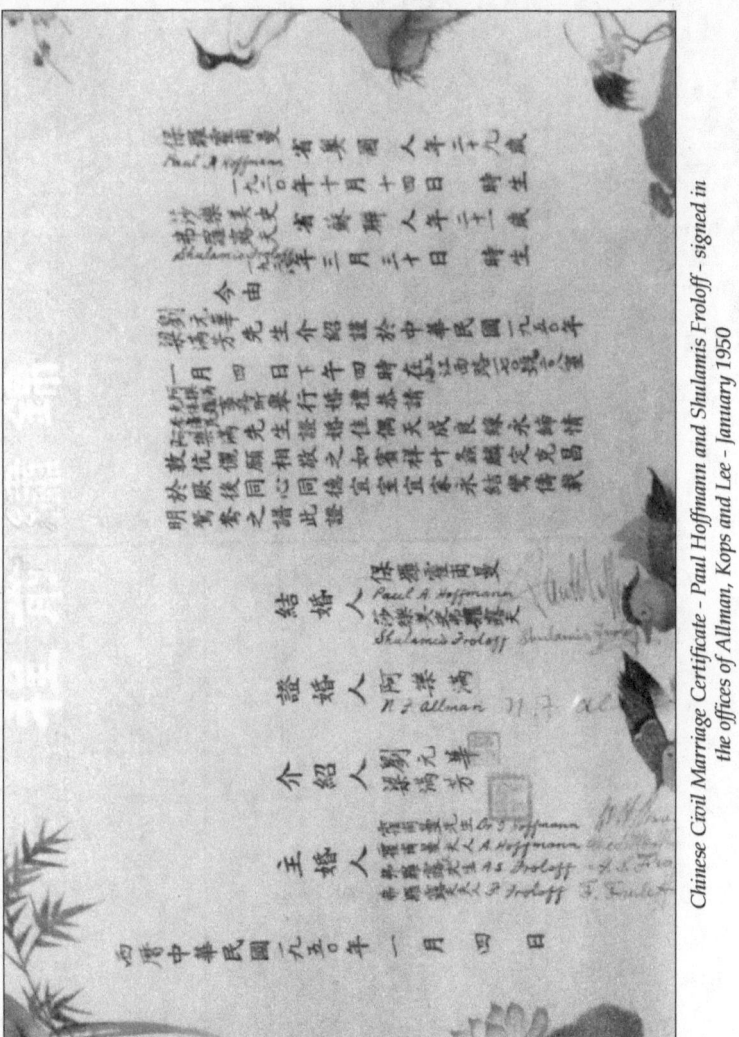

Chinese Civil Marriage Certificate - Paul Hoffmann and Shulamis Froloff - signed in the offices of Allman, Kops and Lee - January 1950

SHALAMA

Shanghai Gas Company circa 1950 - Shalama seated ninth from left

Entrance to the Brooklyn Court Apartment on Route des Soeurs in Shanghai where the Froloffs lived 1940 -1951 (Photographed in 2022 by T. Kanagaratnam)

Shalama with servant and pets at the Allman Fah Hwa House - 1950

Shalama with her parents, Fanya and Avram, at the Allman House - Winter 1950/1951

SHALAMA

Paul on the Egypt Excursion on the way to Marseille - April 1952

JEAN HOFFMANN LEWANDA

Shirley, Paul and Paul's sister Licci with two-year-old Abe, newborn Jeanie and Licci's nine-year-old son Jack - Boston 1954

*Exhibit of wedding related artifacts at the Shanghai Jewish Refugees Museum - 2023
The two silver serving items on the right were wedding gifts Shalama and Paul
received in March of 1950*

Bibliography

Ben-Canaan, Dan. *Jewish Footprints in Harbin: Concise Historical Notes.* Heilongiang Education Press, 2018.

Ben-Canaan, Dan. *Tombstone Histories: Tales of Jewish Life in Harbin.* Earnshaw Books, 2023.

Berkenwald, Leah. "Laura Margolis: The Heroine of Shanghai." *Jewish Women's Archive,* 3 Mar. 2022, https://jwa.org/blog/laura-margolis-heroine-of-shanghai

Beth-Hatefutsoth, The Nahum Goldmann Museum of the Jewish Diaspora. *Exhibit Guide: Passage Through China: The Jewish Communities of Harbin, Tientsin and Shanghai.* Tel Aviv, Summer, 1986

BREM Archives. *(Bureau for Affairs of Russian Emigrants in Manchurian Empire)* "File on Abram Froloff." Khabarovsk State Archive, Russia. 1938-1939. https://gakhkkhabarai.ru/projects/brem/41043/?sphrase_id=1882

Bulletin. Igud Yotzei Sin: Association of Former Residents of China. *English Supplement.* Issue No. 362, Feb-Mar 2000; Issue No. 363, Apr-May 2000; Issue No. 368, May-June 2001; Issue No. 373, Sept-Oct 2002; Vol. LV, Issue No. 396, July-August 2008; Vol. LVIII, No. 404, April-May 2011; Vol. LVI, Issue No. 400, Nov-Dec 2009; Vol. LVIX, Issue No. 407, April-May 2011; Vol. 58, Issue No. 406, Nov-Dec 2011; Vol. LVX, Issue No. 408, Aug-Sept 2012

Clurman, Irene, and Dan Ben-Canaan. "A Brief History of the Jews of Harbin: How a Manchurian Fishing Village Became a Railroad Town and A Haven for Jews." *JewishGen KehilaLinks,* 16 July 2019, https://kehilalinks.jewishgen.org/

harbin?Brief_History.htm

Council on the Jewish Experience in Shanghai (CJES). *Refuge in Shanghai*. Newsletter: *Special "Rickshaw Reunion"* Edition, April 1997

Dvir, Yoad. "Chief Rabbi and Spiritual Leader of the Jewish Community in Harbin." *Bulletin: Igud Yotzei Sin-Association of the Former Residents of China English Supplement,* vol. LVIII, no. 401, Apr-May 2011, pp.47-58

Earnshaw, Graham. *Tales of Old Shanghai:The Glorious Past of China's Greatest City.* Earnshaw Books, 2012.

French, Paul, *The Old Shanghai A-Z.* Hong Kong University Press, 2010.

Hoffmann, Paul. *Witness to History: From Vienna to Shanghai-A Memoir of Escape, Survival and Resilience.* Earnshaw Books, 2021

Hongkew Chronicle. *Newsletter of the Reunion '80 Committee.* Vol. 4, No. 3, Fall 1985;

Vol. 6, No.2, Summer 1987; Vol 7, No. 1, Spring 1988; Vol. 6, No. 4, Winter/1987/1988

Horn, Dara. *People Love Dead Jews: Reports from a Haunted Present.* W.W. Norton & Company, 2021, Chapter 2: *Frozen Jews,* pp. 15-47

Houguangbing: Editor. "The Most Serious Flood of the Songhua River Basin in Nearly a hundred years happened in 1932." IKCEST. 03 June 2018, http://wwww.ikcest.org/index.htm

Israel-China Voice of Friendship. *Activities of the Israel-China Friendship Society.* Israel-China Friendship Society in Tel-Aviv, No. 30, February-Mar 2000; *On the Friendship Path with China.* No. 72, Apr-May 2011; No. 73, Aug-Sept 2011; *The Israel-China Friendship Society-20 Years-Challenges for the Future,* No. 75, Apr-May 2012

Liberman, Yaacov. *My China: Jewish Life in the Orient 1900-1950.*

Gefen Publishing House, 1998

Perlstrauss, Sophie. *Hometown Shanghai*. Self-published, 2003.

Samson, Mary. *My Remarkable Journey*. Self-published, 2012.

Shichor, Yiitzhak. "*Betar China: The impact of a Remote Jewish Movement, 1929-1949.*" *Jerusalem Center for Public Affairs*, vol. 32, nos. 3-4, 19 Aug. 2021, https://jcpa.org/article/betar-china-the-impact-of-a-remote-jewish-youth-movement-1929-1949/

Vladimirsky, Irena. "The Jews of Harbin." *Museum of the Jewish People at Beit Hatfutsot,*19 Aug 2019, https://www.bh.org.il/jews-harbin/.

Wikipedia. "Harbin." *Wikipedia*. 28 January 2022, https://en.wikipedia.org/wiki/Harbin.

About The Author

Jean Hoffmann Lewanda was born in New York City in 1954, one year after her parents, Paul and Shulamis Hoffmann, arrived in the United States, after escaping communist China in February of 1952. In 2021 Jean published her father's post-mortem memoir *Witness to History – From Vienna to Shanghai: A Memoir of Escape, Survival and Resilience*. The overwhelming interest and response to *Witness to History* was the inspiration for this work of historical fiction which highlights the lives of the Jewish Russian community that lived in China for almost six decades.

Jean attended the University at Albany, New York University and the University of Connecticut. Now retired from teaching, her forty year career as a special educator included students from preschool to adulthood. Jean resides in Yardley, Pennsylvania. She continues to research the Jewish Chinese experience and participate in Holocaust awareness programs by sharing her family story.

www.ingramcontent.com/pod-product-compliance
Lightning Source LLC
LaVergne TN
LVHW030318070526
838199LV00069B/6494